Fabric & Form

IRISH FASHION SINCE 1950

For
ÚNA, CIARA
AND ROSIE

GENERAL INFORMATION

This book accompanies an Ulster Museum exhibition. The Ulster Museum is one of Great Britain's national museums and has been described as 'the mother museum' of Northern Ireland. The vast permanent collections cover a rich variety of material – fine and applied art, archaeology and ethnography, local history, botany, zoology and geology. The Museum also offers an extensive annual programme of temporary exhibitions, lectures, films, workshops and events.

Dates of exhibition

The Ulster Museum, Belfast
25 October 1996 – 9 February 1997
The National Museum of Ireland, Dublin
March – August 1997

Fabric & Form

IRISH FASHION SINCE 1950

ELIZABETH MCCRUM

Picture Research by Victoria Wilkes

SUTTON PUBLISHING

ULSTER MUSEUM

First published in the United Kingdom in 1996
Sutton Publishing Ltd
Phoenix Mill · Thrupp · Stroud · Gloucestershire · GL5 2BU
in association with
Ulster Museum · Botanic Gardens · Belfast · BT9 5AB

British Library Cataloguing in Publication Data
A catalogue record for this book is available from the British Library.

ISBN 0-7509-1286-3

*Cover pictures: Left, hat by Philip Treacy (1993); Right, top to bottom, details of outfits by Louise Kennedy (1994), Irene Gilbert (1953), Lainey Keogh (1994), Michael Mortell (1985); Background, dress fabric by Sybil Connolly (*c. *1960).*

Typeset in 11/14½ Sabon.
Typesetting and origination by
Sutton Publishing Limited.
Printed in Great Britain by
Butler & Tanner, Frome, Somerset.

CONTENTS

LIST OF ILLUSTRATIONS

Colour Plates

Black and White Plates

ACKNOWLEDGEMENTS

There are few secondary sources dealing with Irish fashion apart from consistently good and useful, but usually brief, articles in newspapers and magazines. Much of the research for this book has therefore been dependent on information directly gleaned from as wide a variety as possible of people involved in fashion in Ireland. Although all of these were very busy, all gave their time and information most generously and supportively.

All the designers, over seventy in number, mentioned in the book have been very generous with their help. They are all due my thanks for their information, advice and other assistance. In many cases their personal assistants have been more than helpful in sending back-up information, photographs, etc.

The designers have been supported loyally and consistently by the excellent Irish fashion press, past and present. I would particularly thank Gabrielle Williams and Robert O'Byrne of the *Irish Times*, Deirdre McQuillan of the *Sunday Tribune*, Terry Keane of the *Sunday Independent*, Ita Hines, and also Paula Reed of *The Sunday Times*, Felicity Green of the *Daily Telegraph*, Godfrey Deeney of *Uomo Vogue*, Carolyn McGrath of *Image*, Sara Foote of *IT* and Jane Mulvagh for their help.

All the photographers who provided the illustrations have also been very helpful and supportive. A wide variety of others with individual involvement in Irish fashion must also be thanked and are as follows: Cecily McMenanim, Catherine Condell and Deirdre Kelly of Brown Thomas; Oonagh Moriarty of Blarney Woollen Mills; Geraldine Waldron of Clery's; Suzanne McDougald; Marguerite McCurtain; Peter Crown of Lachasse; Moya Donnellan; Winnie Cunningham of the Design Centre; Dr Brian Hill of the Department of Design and Industry, University of Ulster; Mrs Cathleen Murphy; The Earl and Countess of Rosse; The Countess of Snowdon; Mrs Phyllis Seigne; Richard Gorman; Richard Clarke; Mary McLaughlin of RTE's *Head 2 Toe*; Eddie Shanahan; the Press Office, Aer Lingus; Kate Franklyn; Peter Hope Lumley; Patricia Jorgensen; M. Christian

Lacroix; Gabrielle Lingle of Smurfit Management Services, Monte Carlo; Leontia Fetherston of PLPR Consultants, Anna Mooney of Franklyn Creative Consultants; Brid Rosney; Joanne Taylor of Guinness; Barbara Kavanagh and Maura McConnell of RTE's *Late Late Show;* Linda McHugh of the Irish Linen Guild; Diana Fisher of the White House Historical Association; Patricia Keilthy of Limerick Regional Technical College; Olive Clegg, ex-Head of Textiles and Fashion at the University of Ulster; Frances McDonough of the National College of Art and Design; Punam McGookin; Jim Mawhinney of the Clothing Development Council, Belfast; Michelle Shirlowe of LEDU; Rose Mary Craig and Lorraine Egan of The Irish Trade Board; Leonora Curry. Fabric and thread manufacturers who have very kindly helped are Jackie Best and John England of John England; Brian Hazard of Blacker's Mill (Castleisland); John McNutt of John McNutt Ltd; Joan Mooney and Donald Pratt of Avoca Handweavers; Derek Bailie, Ian McMorris, and Noel McEvoy of Ulster Weavers; Gail Kelly of Herdmans Ltd.

Colleagues at my own and other institutions have given great help. These include the late John Teahan, Colleen Dube and Mairead Dunlevy of the National Museum of Ireland; Valerie Wilson of the Ulster Folk and Transport Museum and Sally FitzMaurice of Rothe House, Kilkenny, and my colleagues in the Division of Art at the Ulster Museum, particularly Dr S.B. Kennedy. Bill Anderson Porter and Michael McKeown of the Ulster Museum Photographic Department took all the photographs of Ulster Museum specimens which appear in this book. Sandra Neill and Paula Talbot of the Ulster Museum Marketing Department gave welcome help. Elise Taylor and Kim Mawhinney of my own Department of Applied Art have given constant help and encouragement, and taken workloads off me as far as possible. Mary Dornan has typed and retyped my manuscript.

In particular Victoria Wilkes' contribution to this book must be very gratefully acknowledged. She has been responsible for all picture research and copyright work involved in its publication, which in a book of this nature has been a full-time and complex job. Her contribution is much appreciated.

I owe gratitude to Leonora Curry and Olive Clegg who have kindly and helpfully read the text of this book.

My husband, Ted Hickey, has engendered, encouraged and helped edit this book, and my daughters Úna, Ciara and Rosaleen have put up with my preoccupation with it. I give them all my thanks.

Elizabeth McCrum

INTRODUCTION

In the international arena Ireland's contribution has always been of far greater significance than either her small population or her location on the far periphery of the political mainstream might seem to warrant. She has, one need only remember, at different times sent her religion, her literature and her population into the world through the early Christian missionaries to Europe, the work of nineteenth- and twentieth-century Irish writers and the nineteenth and twentieth-century Irish diaspora. In short, to paraphrase a comment of Saki, she has 'produced more culture than can be consumed locally', and as a consequence she has a far higher cultural profile than many larger countries.

Dress is an integral part of the identity of any society. The history of Irish dress is a constantly changing amalgam of prevailing cultural, political, economic, aesthetic and technical influences as is that of any dynamic society. Periodically, however, these have fused to produce a recognizably distinct mode of dress and there have been certain consistent strands running through the last two thousand years or so of Irish costume. One has been the production for the home and export market of weatherproof wools; another has been a love of fine linen, and a third has been a taste for fine and finely embellished, brightly coloured materials. The cloth of Ireland has been a crucial part of the dress of the country. It has been the fabric of the country too that gave rise to the first international showing of Irish fashion around 1950, and has periodically ever since been its main inspiration.

Fashion is one of the most vital of the applied arts, an immediate indicator of changing tastes, perceptions and technology. For the purposes of this book it can be defined further as the type of clothing which, originating in the late medieval courts of Western Europe, conferred status not only by fineness of make and fabric but, most characteristically, by the continual supercession of one style by another. This last distinctive feature has always had as a prerequisite a relatively stable but mobile society, with, typically, a powerful middle class poised to move into the upper classes. The constant changes of fashion provided, and still provide, a means of keeping one step ahead of emulators.

'Irish' fashion is discussed here in relation to its place in mainstream Western European fashion. What makes it particularly worthy of study, however, is its very distinctive features and idiosyncratic style within this context. No other country of relative size has, in the economic period since the Second World War, so successfully and so consistently performed this juggling act of combining global requirements of style and finish with undeniably national characteristics. It is this combination of outward and inward attitudes, of looking to one's own culture in order to appeal to an international market, that distinguishes late twentieth-century Irish fashion.

Designers or companies who have or had a high national or international profile, and who therefore have had influence on the development of fashion at home and abroad are the chief subjects of this study. They work at the top level of the extensive clothing industry in Ireland and this must also be considered.

It is hoped that this book, in describing, evaluating and accounting for the phenomenon which is Irish Fashion, will be a useful source book for students and those with a general interest in the subject. If it sparks off further research and further increases government realization of the fact that economically and aesthetically fashion is far from frivolous, but is the vital trail-blazing aspect of a huge industry, so much the better.

1 EARLY TRADITIONS: UP TO 1950

BACKGROUND

Irish fashion since 1950 owes much of its distinctive quality to a remarkable fidelity to the forms and fabrics of earlier periods. Thus any account of contemporary fashion needs to have this historic context properly evaluated. Of the four main natural fabrics – wool, linen, silk and cotton – only cotton does not manifest itself in an immediately recognizable Irish version. It is worth pointing out that until the second half of the twentieth century, cloth was, to use Alison Lurie's phrase, 'the primary worldly good', an expensive and much-prized commodity. The quality, quantity and hue of the cloth in a garment were fundamental to its worth. The lavish use of distinctively finished and coloured cloth by the Irish was as much a source of irritation to the sixteenth-century English colonists as their alien styles of dress. Respect for fine cloth was universal, but it would seem that it was particularly and consistently highly prized in Ireland, as contemporary comments testify. The embellishments of dress – lace, crochet and embroidery – also have readily recognizable Irish versions, some of which also have a long pedigree.

An account of historic forms of dress, highlighting those which had contemporary or later national or even international influence will follow the description of the fabrics from which they were made. Some of these garments such as nineteenth-century traditional dress – the dress of the isolated rural poor – and, most notably, early Aran knitwear had direct influence on late twentieth-century fashion designers. In other cases the earlier forms are of interest more as examples of the type of garment for which the cloth is always particularly suited.

FABRICS

Wool

Wool has been woven in Ireland since at least the late Bronze Age. The earliest surviving piece, from County Antrim, dating from *c.* 750 BC,

'[The Irish] are delighted in simple light colours, as red and yellow'

FYNES MORYSON, 1600[1]

already shows considerable weaving skill. Irish woollen cloth was successfully exported from medieval times. This healthy trade was crippled, unfortunately, at the end of the seventeenth century, when the English, fearing for their own woollen industry, prohibited the export of Irish wool except to England, and then levied taxes on it. Trade was later further damaged by the high output of newly industrialized countries in the nineteenth century. The difficulties of urban wool weavers, who produced standard wares of flannel, worsted, superfine etc. were considerable but are not part of this story. It was the survival and development of the homespun products of the equally hardpressed rural weavers which is crucial as far as late twentieth century Irish fashion is concerned.

PLATE 1 The Dungiven costume, early seventeenth century. Exact replicas of the jacket, trews and mantle discovered near Dungiven, Co. Derry in 1956, made to show how the originals would have looked. The jacket shows considerable tailoring skill, but the trews and cloak are much worn and patched.
Collection Ulster Museum

During much of the nineteenth century famine, trade barriers, seasonal emigration and, above all, poverty hampered the development of home weaving even where it had been traditionally strong, such as in Donegal. Individuals, through private schemes, intervened to help the trade from time to time, but it was the creation of the Congested Districts Board in 1891 which proved of most help in turning the tide of rural poverty in the west of Ireland. 'Congested Districts' were areas where scattered rural populations of high density had virtually nothing to sustain them. The Board aimed to develop agriculture, forestry, animal breeding, weaving, spinning, fishing and other potential rural industries. In 1893 it combined with the Irish Industries Association. Direct help was given, for example, to weavers in the Ardara district of Donegal who received loans of new looms and aid with marketing. Financial help was also given to those aiming to set up a new industry. The Providence Woollen Mill (still working) at Foxford, Co. Mayo, started by the Sisters of Charity, was helped in this way, and was soon a much hailed success. This being a mechanized industry it provided invaluable work for the female work force, who could not work the heavy hand-operated looms as easily as men.

The revival of the tweed industry was largely due to its suitability to garments worn for the newly fashionable sporting, country and travelling activities of the mid-nineteenth century. Previously, fashionable people would not have exposed themselves to the elements to the extent that they needed stylish waterproof and weatherproof outfits. Donegal tweed began to be exported as a uniquely Irish cloth to France, England and America by Logue of Killybegs and Magees of Donegal Town among others. When fashion and lifestyles changed after the First World War, however, quality and demand fell and the industry declined again. The Congested Districts Board was dissolved in 1923, but the Gaeltacht Services Division of the Department of Lands helped take up its mantle in 1930 and reorganized the handwoven tweed industry. The Division made a policy decision to use machine-spun instead of homespun yarn, to make a finer quality, more standard cloth, and also to market the product itself. It established a marketing depot, which became Gaeltarra Eireann in 1957, and Údarás na Gaeltachta in 1980. A spinning plant established at Kilcar in 1950 kept the industry fed with yarn. New markets were developed and when fashion turned in its favour again after the Second World War the industry was in a position to take full advantage of this.

As for clothes made from wool, the most distinctive and much remarked-upon item of clothing from pre-Christian times until the seventeenth century was the woollen 'brat' or large, voluminous, enveloping, weatherproof 'cloak-wrap' mantle, as Mairead Dunlevy[2] defines it. Its form and colour could vary according to the class and pocket of the owner, and to the period, but its function and voluminous form remained constant. As a 'brat' it was four-cornered and was described as very colourful and embellished with gold as worn by the aristocracy in Conor mac Nessa's time, in the fourth century. After several variations it developed to a mantle shape by the sixteenth century. By this time it could be lined, unlined or, most typically, napped until the curled, tufted surface resembled fur. The extant, so-called 'Mantle of Saint Brighid', now in Brussels, and probably dating to the eleventh century, shows this tufted effect.

These mantles were exported to south-west England and Wales and also to the Continent, where 'Hibernian Cloaks' were much prized. The English, despite their disdain for native Irish dress, had to admit its practicality as a 'garment by day and a house by night'.[4]

Before the twentieth-century phenomenon of completely effective waterproofing of cloth, the weatherproof qualities of properly fulled and napped wool were more highly regarded than now, when the *warmth* of wool is its chief association. Irish mantles were issued to the English army in Ireland in 1600 because 'being never so wet [the mantles] will presently with a little shaking and wringing be presently dry'.[5]

Other types of woollen dress of the sixteenth and seventeenth centuries which have survived, usually preserved through immersion in a bog, show considerable tailoring skills in construction, and also ingenuity in solving such problems as gathering the heavy cloth without undue bulk.

It was not until the mid-nineteenth century that woollen garments were exported again in significant quantity from Ireland. The qualities described above combined in the form of the well-tailored, weatherproof 'Ulster'.[6] This was a caped travelling coat originally

'They have woollen jackets, but very short; plain breeches close to their thighs; and over these they cast their mantles or shag-rugs . . . fringed with an agreeable mixture of colours, in which they wrap themselves up and sleep upon the bare ground.'

WILLIAM GOOD, *1566*[3]

PLATE 2 Drawing of Irish soldiers and 'poor people', by Albrecht Dürer, 1521. Dürer's depiction of drapery was especially admired by his contemporaries. His interest in drawing these figures was probably aroused as much by the unusual fabrics as by the style of the dress. Courtesy of the National Gallery of Ireland

made and sold by McGee and Company of 30–40 High Street, Belfast, a successful tailoring and outfitting firm which specialized in overcoats. The greatcoat or surtout, the standard overcoat, was heavy and cumbersome, and when John Getty McGee launched his 'Ulster' in 1866 its success was almost instantaneous. It was a less bulky but remarkably weatherproof coat of Irish frieze – the cloth was often napped and curled in a manner reminiscent of the Irish mantle. It was cut close at the chest, originally with a hood and later with a shoulder cape, and many useful pockets, As one advertisement put it, 'it caused the word "Ulster" to be imported into every language in the civilized world'. A version for women was produced from the early 1870s and the Ulster remained popular at home and abroad until the advent of the enclosed motor car spelt redundancy for these heavy coats, which could weigh nearly two stone (12.7 kg).

PLATE 3 An advertisement for McGee's 'Ulster' overcoat. Reproduced in Jack McCoy's article, Irish Arts Review, *Winter 1985*

Wool, as the most readily available and cheap material, produced most of the traditional forms of Irish dress. Many of these are the fossilized survivals of more general Western European fashions, which having arrived in isolated communities and having proved to be suitable for local conditions, ceased to become fashion and became traditional 'Irish' rural dress. Examples include the red flannel petticoat which is a survival of a seventeenth-century Western European fashion and the nineteenth-century swallow-tail coat and knee breeches which were eighteenth-century survivors, as was the hooded cloak, known as

PLATE 4 Mac Swiney and company at an al fresco *dinner, John Derricke, c. 1581. An interesting illustration of Irish habits also shows the contemporary shaggy mantle ; the voluminously sleeved linen shirts, worn under short woollen jackets with very short pleated skirts and open seamed sleeves; and the tooled leather jacket (worn by the chieftain Mac Swiney)*

the Kinsale Cloak, which survived in Cork until very recently. Only the Aran islanders' dress which included wide trousers, woven belt (*crois*), sleeved waistcoat, heavy double-breasted waistcoat, and *bainin*, a white flannel collarless jacket, appears to be an original sartorial response to local conditions. The *bainin* was worn in other West Coast areas as well as on Aran. These garments have spawned fashionable progeny in the latter half of the twentieth century.

The most famous form of Irish wool, the Aran sweater, perceived as a quintessentially Irish garment, has had a curious history. Once thought of as of great antiquity, it is a twentieth-century development, a proof of the power of wishful thinking and sales strategy. It exemplifies the dictum, 'When the legend becomes fact, print the legend.'[7]

Knitting was first introduced to Ireland in the seventeenth century, and was another of the skills promoted by the Congested Districts Board in 1893. In the 1890s it was taken up most extensively in Donegal. On the Aran islands at that time it seems to have been limited to the domestic production of socks. Within thirty years, however, this situation had so much changed that by about the late 1920s virtuoso knitters had invented an exuberant variety of over seventy Aran stitches.

This extraordinary development seems mainly to have been due initially to outside influences. The Congested District Board's improvement of fishing facilities brought fishermen from outside areas such as Scotland and the Channel Islands to the Aran Islands for the fishing season. The blue jerseys or ganseys of the British and Scottish fishermen were adopted in the early twentieth century by the young fishermen of Aran who called them *geansais* – significantly there is no Irish word for sweater or jumper before this borrowing of 'gansey'. These garments had simple cabling designs only on the upper chest area. It seems likely that the fishermen's wives who accompanied their husbands, to gut the fish they caught, taught the principle of cabling to the islanders. The island knitters thus had the crucial technique they needed to give scope to their inventiveness.

Initially the idiosyncratic white jumpers with complex stitches were made for young boys, usually for their first communion. Extra inspiration was received when emigrants to the Boston area returned to Aran in the early years of the century. They brought back knitting patterns copied from immigrants from other countries, probably from Central Europe or perhaps Scandinavia.

By the mid-1930s Aran sweaters were sold in 'The Country Shop' in Dublin. The brainchild of the remarkable Dr Muriel Gahan, founder of 'The Irish Countrywomen's Association', it opened in 1930 to sell and promote traditional crafts. In the late 1930s the commercial production of Aran sweaters began when a number of mostly Galway-based companies, notably O'Maille's, supplied materials to Aran sweaters and sold the finished products. Catherine Ryan began to buy Aran sweaters for her shop, 'Cleo', which opened in 1936.[8] As her daughter, Kathleen Joyce, who now runs the business, remembers, they had 'gorgeous patterns, but some crazy shapes'. By the 1950s, Aran sweaters were sent to the US – exports to America were worth £25,000 in 1952 – and the shapes began to be standardized, thanks to the efforts of designers like Maureen Evans, who worked for Kennedy's of Ardara. By now the light cream 'bainin' Aran was the accepted form, and was chunkier than formerly, as double knitting wool was used more often than the earlier finer wools. Printed Aran patterns became available, Donegal knitters gave up their traditional Fair Isle knitting for Aran and the mythology of Aran knitting's antiquity began to take hold. One of the contributory factors to the myth of Aran knitting was a misinterpretation of lines from J.M. Synge's short play *Riders to the Sea* (1904) in which the body of a young fisherman, washed ashore far away, is identified by a bit of flannel shirt and a stocking sent to

PLATE 5 Group of Aran Islanders, c. 1910. All are wearing fishermen's 'ganseys', which if decorated at all only have simple decorative stitching on the upper chest area. The 'Aran' sweater, with its rich variety of stitches, had not yet developed.
© National Museum of Ireland

his sisters. Tim Robinson, in his book *Stones of Aran: Labyrinth* (1995), wryly observed that when one of Jean Paul Gaultier's male models paraded in tight-fitting Aran trousers, sweater and cap in snow-white wool in 1985, it was 'an outfit that certainly would have identified him had he been washed ashore drowned'.[9]

The myth was given further credence by Dr Heinz Edgar Kiewe in his book *The Sacred History of Knitting* (1967), a curious work which connected Aran knitting work to Biblical times. However, with or without Dr Kiewe's help, the stage was now set for the successful development of the Irish knitwear trade.

PLATE 6 The Killarney guide, from Mr and Mrs S.C. Hall's 'Ireland, its Scenery, Character etc' (1843). The cutaway coat, knee breeches and brogues are all sartorial survivors of an earlier period.

Linen

Linen is also very closely associated with Ireland. Although worked by man since *c.* 7000 BC, and worked on an industrial scale, in Egypt, since *c.* 4000 BC, it was not in wide use in Ireland until much later. It may have been introduced by the trading Phoenicians. Brehon laws enforced the cultivation of flax, and by the fourteenth century linen was exported to England. Its ecclesiastical use was well established as was its use for shirts and underwear. From surviving Irish medieval sources it is difficult to distinguish whether tunics were linen or wool, but by the sixteenth century linen was worn by the

PLATE 7 Hooded cloak from Co. Cork. The hooded cloak, worn until recently in parts of Co. Cork, was very widely worn in Ireland in the nineteenth century. It was derived from similar cloaks, worn throughout Europe in the eighteenth and early nineteenth centuries but which then elsewhere passed from use. © National Museum of Ireland

native Irish in a distinctive and well-documented way. Voluminous long shirts which were tucked up at the waist with long hanging sleeves were worn with very short, tooled-leather jerkins or woollen jackets with short pleated skirts (*see* plate 2).

They were typically dyed yellow with the prized saffron dye, which was thought to protect the body from the dangers of unwashed cloth. Sumptuary legislation of 1537 tried to reduce the yardage needed for a shirt from 25–35 yards (23–32 metres) – the range being needed to differentiate social status – to 12–16 yards (11–15 metres), and to ban saffron dye. Although the success of this legislation was at the time limited, these exuberant styles barely survived into the seventeenth century as the English conquest was completed. Linen once again became reduced to underwear and only the linen headdresses of women, maintaining earlier styles, continued to excite comment about their idiosyncrasy.

Linen was not worn as outerwear again until the eighteenth century. This came about through the popularity of Indian chintz, (washable cotton fabric dyed with fast colours), which became so fashionable as a dress fabric that cotton printing was set up in England. Silk and woollen producers, fearing for their livelihood, obtained the imposition of excise duties on Indian imports, and, by 1721, the prohibition of the import and sale, and also of the use and wear of all printed cottons, except for export. The English printers evaded this by printing on linen or linen/cotton mixes, which gave a great boost to the Irish and Scottish linen trades. Many ships from Belfast took linen to London which was printed there and then re-imported. Soon, from the 1750s, linen was printed in Ireland, at Donnybrook, Leixlip and Drumcondra. An Act of 1774 eventually lifted the ban on the home sale of printed all-cotton goods, though imports were still prohibited. By the 1780s cottons too were printed in Ireland. Printed linens and cottons were by then fashionable as 'undress' (informal) wear.

The crucial social importance of this development was that the garments could be washed, which raised public awareness of, and regard for, hygiene. Linen washed very well. Its great wet strength has always made it the most durable fabric particularly when heavy or frequent washing is needed, hence its perennial use for underwear.

When the fashion for printed linen and cotton diminished, cotton took over as the dominant dress fabric during the early years of the nineteenth century. Cotton spinning and weaving threatened the domestic, low-key eighteenth century linen industry in Ireland, but when linen production, particularly of fine linen and damask, became heavily industrialized in the north of Ireland in the nineteenth century, Irish linen was exported and became known all over the world. It was still used primarily for household purposes, underwear and shirts, since unless it was heavily and frequently starched it creased too much for dress use. Exceptions to this rule were its occasional use for summer wear. The Ulster Museum has an unbleached linen outfit of the 1880s which belonged to the wife of John Dunlop, the inventor of India rubber tyres.

After the sewing machine became readily available associated developments such as the shirtmaking industry of Londonderry grew to vast proportions. By 1902 factory workers and outworkers were producing 'sixty thousand dozen' (720,000) shirts per week. The separate collar industry exported 20 million collars annually by 1912.

The linen industry was in decline by 1950. Competition from cotton, rayon, paper tableware, nylon and other manmade fibres, political developments which led to diminished markets and cheap

'Their shirts be very strange,
not reaching past the thigh:
with pleats on pleats they pleated are as thick as pleats may lie.
Whose sleeves hang trailing down almost onto the shoe:'
JOHN DERRICKE[10]

PLATE 8 Printed linen morning robe, c. 1785. Wood blocks and hand painting were still used to produce the pattern on this dress, although copper-plate printing had already developed in Ireland.
© National Museum of Ireland

PLATE 9 Irish Kern (footsoldiers) drawn from life by an unknown artist, pre-1547, which effectively illustrates the lavish use of fabric in the linen shirts as well as the short, tooled-leather jackets of the time. Ashmolean Museum, Oxford

competitive imports, reduced the demand for linen. The post-1950 requirements of fashion have, however, partially and periodically helped reverse this trend.

Silk

Silk was worn in Ireland from about the tenth century, but it was not, of course, an indigenous fabric nor ever became one, despite some experiments with breeding silk worms. It was woven in Ireland from the early seventeenth century in the Coombe and Pimlico districts of Dublin. Huguenots swelled the weavers' numbers in the late seventeenth century after the Revocation of the Edict of Nantes, and also in the mid-eighteenth century, helped by the Society for the Relief of French Protestants. Despite government help, administered by the Dublin Society,[11] and attempts to encourage court wear of Irish fabric, the industry declined due to the fashion for linen and cotton in the late eighteenth century, the loss of court functions after the Act of Union of 1800, and the sharp rise in the price of raw silk in 1809. Irish silk was always potentially undermined by the lure of French and English imports, mostly seen as more prestigious sources of what was a particularly expensive fabric. A more thriving aspect of silk weaving was the production of poplin, traditionally started by David Dignes de la Touche in the late seventeenth century. Both furnishing and dress poplins were made, the latter having a wool weft and silk warp. Plain and watered silk poplin has now become a naturalized Irish fabric, and is still used to complement Irish lace or crochet, which it does most effectively. Poplin manufacture is also now in decline. The Ulster

PLATE 10 Formal silk open robe and petticoat, c. 1785. The silk is by William Williams, recorded as a Dublin silk weaver or manufacturer 1782–1805. A pattern of this dress silk appears in his sample book. © National Museum of Ireland

Museum collection contains a beautiful evening outfit of olive-green watered and plain poplin made for Mrs Maeve Ryan by Ib Jorgensen from one of the last bolts of fabric produced by Elliott's.[12]

PLATE 11 Outfit by Ib Jorgensen, 1964, made from one of the last bolts of poplin produced by Thomas Elliott and Sons, a long-established Dublin poplin weaving firm. The wonderful texture of this fabric can here be seen to advantage.
Collection Ulster Museum

Embroidery, Lace and Crochet

The traditional embellishments of cloth in Ireland have impacted on the late twentieth century development of Irish fashion. Most of these enterprises began in the nineteenth century as means to relieve poverty and give opportunity of wage earning to women, and then developed as successful small industries. Embroidery centres, started in the 1820s, led to many women working for the Glasgow-based firms making 'Ayrshire' embroidery, white thread work on muslin. When this trade declined, the women turned to embroidering locally woven linen. This tradition of embroidery persists, particularly in the north of Ireland.

The making of Limerick lace (tambour or needlerun embroidery on machine-made net) and Carrickmacross lace (appliqued cambric on machine net with needlepoint filling stitches) were both started in the 1820s and gave much needed female employment in their areas. The fortunes of these industries were mixed until the 1880s when lace became used in quantity as a trimming for fashionable dress, and demand for both products rose. Crochet too was introduced to Ireland after the Great Famine as relief work by the Ursuline Sisters in Blackrock, Co. Cork and by Mrs Roberts of Thornton, Co. Kildare, and Mrs Hand in Clones, Co. Monaghan, and by the 1860s it was an established cottage industry. By 1900 it too was exported in quantity as dress trimming. In the early twentieth century complete garments were formed from crochet. It was known as *point d'Irlande* and was, for a time, patronized by French designers, notably Paquin.

After the First World War, all these industries declined again until fashion claimed them once more. Crochet and Carrickmacross lace in particular were adopted and again given a high international profile by late twentieth-century Irish fashion designers.

The Celtic Revival's influence on embroidery was seen from the early 1880s, when Kells embroidery, made in Donegal under the aegis of the Donegal Industrial Fund, was started by Mrs Ernest Hart in 1883. This used motifs from the Books of Kells, Durrow and Lindisfarne. Of more lasting influence was the work of the Dun Emer Guild,[14] set up to produce Irish craftwork, which had links with the Irish literary movement and the Arts and Crafts movement. The Dun Emer Guild was founded in 1902 by the artist Evelyn Gleeson who invited the two Yeats sisters, Lily and Elizabeth, to join her. Lily had worked as an embroideress with William Morris's daughter May, and was responsible

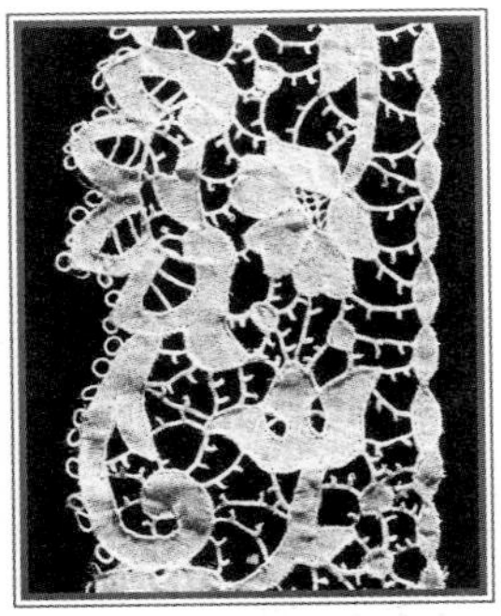

PLATE 12 *Detail of a Carrickmacross lace border, late nineteenth century. This distinctive Irish lace is typically made from fine muslin applied to net, embellished with needlepoint stitches. The lace can also be made without the net underlay.* Collection Ulster Museum

for the Guild's embroidery output. Banners, vestments and household articles formed the bulk of the production, but both the Dun Emer Guild and Cuala Industries, set up in 1908 by the Yeats sisters on parting company with Evelyn Gleeson, also produced dress embroidery. Celtic motifs of brightly coloured wool and silk embroidery were used on both fashionable garments and on quasi-historic garments. These motifs became distinctively Irish features of the dress of at least a select group of Irish women, within a mostly fashionable context. They were popular partly because they also fitted in to the aesthetics of the Art Nouveau, Art Deco and Arts and Crafts movements.

The Advance of Fashion

Access to Western European fashion became increasingly available to Irish women from the late eighteenth century onwards. Ireland was by no means as isolated as its geography might suggest. The aristocracy were accustomed to spending part of each year in London and other fashionable centres, and information about the current mode was transmitted by letter, fashion dolls, word of mouth and, from the 1770s on, by fashion magazines. From the early to mid-eighteenth century, newspapers increasingly gave very frequent, detailed and up-to-the-minute accounts of Paris, London and Dublin styles to growing

PLATE 13 *Afternoon dress of crochet, c. 1906–8. Made by the Youghal Co-operative Society Ltd, Co. Cork.* © National Museum of Ireland

PLATE 14 Detail of a cloak by Cuala Industries, c. 1915. A particularly bold detail of brightly coloured pink embroidery which shows a typical floral motif. Collection Ulster Museum

numbers of mostly middle-class readers. Local dressmakers, and, by the end of the nineteenth century, department stores with dressmaking departments and ready-to-wear stock, prided themselves on their knowledge of current trends. People with disposable income, living in any size of town, could keep abreast of fashion. Even the rural poor made attempts at fashionable Sunday best. The wearing of fashionable as opposed to traditional dress marked a very crucial social distinction.

Before the 1950s, Ireland's greatest contribution to the course of international fashion was the Anglo-Irish Captain Edward Molyneux. He was born in London in 1891, but both parents were Irish – his father was from Waterford. He started his fashion career as a sketcher in the London house of Lucile, Lady Duff Gordon. In the First World War he was wounded three times, mentioned twice in dispatches and received the Military Cross. After the war, in 1919, he opened his own house in rue Royale in Paris. His elegant, beautifully cut, discreet clothes had quiet strength of character which contrasted with those of the more exuberant Parisian designers. He had many British clients, including Gertrude Lawrence and Princess Marina, whose wedding dress he made. During the Second World War he successfully worked for the Overseas Board of Trade. He was a founder member of the Incorporated Society of London Fashion Designers. After the war, with Jacques Griffe as his assistant, he returned to work in Paris, but retired in 1950. He made a rather unsuccessful return to the fashion world in 1964. Molyneux had a wide and flamboyant circle of acquaintance in Paris, and owned a very fine collection of French impressionist paintings. He was totally at home in the city which, like Worth, the first true couturier, he had conquered as an outsider.

Molyneux may not have overly stressed his Irish roots but he is a useful indication of the ability of his country to keep producing creative designers of international stature.

PLATE 15 Silk crêpe dress by Edward Molyneux, 1922. Although made at a time when fashion was in a state of flux, this dress displays Molyneux's essential and unfailing elegance. Collection Ulster Museum

2 The American Dream – The 1950s

In the 1950s international fashion focused on the work of the highly talented and powerful Parisian couturiers whose designs were made-to-measure for their rich, elegant clients. The top designers such as Christian Dior every season created the themed look which was eagerly awaited by fashion press, buyers, and manufacturers alike. Elaborate secrecy about the new season's look was maintained until all was revealed at the fashion show, partly to increase the mystique of the occasion and, more practically, to prevent premature copying by mass manufacturers. Fashions percolated downwards from the top levels of society, with very little competition from what would now be known as peer group dressing which then existed only to a very limited extent. Those who were interested looked to the established capitals for inspiration. Paris was the dominant centre of Western European fashion, but buyers and the press also travelled to London, Milan – and to Dublin.[1]

This gives some indication of the international status of the Irish fashion industry at that time. It is even more surprising when seen in the context of the Irish economy as a whole, which at the start of the 1950s was in a poor state, with high unemployment and emigration, poor export figures, low growth and little capital investment in industry. The unhealthy results of years of protectionism were manifest. Heavy tariffs on imports had given home producers, including clothing manufacturers, the advantages of a captive home market, but had also meant that there was no impetus to trade competitively or adopt modern, efficient business practices. It is amazing that despite all this a fashion industry flourished, using indigenous materials and a native workforce to produce goods for which there was a constant and growing export market – in essence a trade board's dream.

Several factors helped bring about this happy situation. Government action in relation to economic planning was obligatory after the application for and receipt of Marshall Aid from the United States, and realistic economic relations with the UK, Europe and the rest of the world had to be initiated. Government measures included the setting up of the Industrial Development Authority, The

Undeveloped Areas Act (which helped textile firms) and Coras Tráchtála, also known as CTT or the 'Dollar Board'. This body, set up in 1951, was particularly important to the development of the fashion industry. A young, energetic staff helped firms to promote their export business and produce the right products for their markets. The export drive concentrated on North America throughout the 1950s and early '60s.

The native fabrics of Ireland were also crucial to the success of Irish fashion, since their innate qualities were a direct source of inspiration to the designers of the time. (This was in accord with Bauhaus design principles with their call for 'truth to materials' and a refinement of line and shape that comes from a strict economy of means and a close study of the nature of materials.) The demands of Irish designers forced the fabric industries to renew and refine the quality of their products. The materials thus produced were in turn adopted and used by international designers – a development which has periodically recurred throughout the latter part of the twentieth century.

The creative and entrepreneurial skills of a new generation of designers, mostly Dublin based, were the third and vital factor which led to the success of Irish fashion in the 1950s.

THE DESIGNERS

Of all of these, the figure who did most to give Irish fashion an international profile was Sybil Connolly. Her designing skills, business acumen and charm were, and continue to be, a formidable combination. She was born in Wales in 1921 to a family which encouraged her design interests and she received brief but intensive dressmaking training at Bradley's of Chepstow Place in London.[2]

After the outbreak of war forced her to leave London, she went to Dublin, where she began to work at 'Richard Alan' for Jack Clarke. His firm had manufactured coats and suits since import tariffs threatened his English manufacturers' agency business. In 1935 he opened his own retail outlet in Grafton Street, 'Richard Alan' (named after his two sons), which thrives to this day. Wishing to start a dress workroom there, he employed Sybil Connolly, initially as its manager rather than as a designer. Meanwhile his coat and suit factory expanded and in 1944 the trade name 'Country Wear' was chosen for its output. By 1947, following contacts made with US and Canadian stores, he began to export to North America. He thus became the trailblazer for the whole Irish clothing export trade.

Meanwhile, Sybil Connolly had ambitions to establish a couture section in what was a ready-to-wear business. The French-Canadian

Gaston Mallet was taken on as designer and his collections, from 1949 to 1952, were well received, proving that an Irish manufacturing company could produce couture quality garments. When he left, Sybil Connolly, who was already doing some design work, took over as house designer. From this time on, the 'Sybil Connolly' label was used for the couture line. The American market in any case preferred a name to a tradename. Her first collection established the pattern of strongly tailored day wear of predominantly Irish tweeds, often of original and custom-made weights and weaves, and highly romantic evening wear (*see* colour plate 3). Although she had had a few models seen at international fashion shows in the US, she first gained wide press coverage there after the influential Philadelphia Fashion Group was brought to see her collection in Dublin in 1952. (This occasion was the first time that CTT helped designers working at this level of fashion.) Her real breakthrough in the American market came when, as a result of this visit, she was invited to show her spring/summer 1953 collection in selected American stores. From her arrival in New York after one of the roughest ever passages of the *Queen Elizabeth*, which in itself gave her and her collection much unexpected publicity, the trip was a personal and professional success which generated an enormous amount of publicity.

The fabrics she used had a particular appeal to the American buyers. These included the strikingly coloured red flannel, bought on the west coast of Ireland, which created her 'Irish Washerwoman' outfit of 1952, fine and fancy weaves of wool and tweeds in new colours specially commissioned from mills and weavers all over Ireland, dyed crochet and lace (notably Carrickmacross), Dublin poplins and other silks, and perhaps Miss Connolly's best-known trademark, pleated handkerchief linen. Nine yards (8 metres) of this very fine Northern Irish linen made one yard (1 metre) of the finished cloth and created a very flattering and uncrushable dress fabric. It was dyed a multitude of subtle and bright colours, and made into classical and timeless evening and cocktail dresses.

'Women should show their curves, not their joints'

SYBIL CONNOLLY

All these distinctively Irish fabrics were turned into garments that were at the cutting edge of mainstream Western European and American fashion developments – the first example of this recurring Irish phenomenon. Miss Connolly was described as 'one of the few designers outside Paris who could launch a line'.[3]

It was during this period, in the mid-1950s, that buyers and journalists who visited France, England and Italy every season added Ireland to their itinerary. Once in Ireland, Miss Connolly treated them to lavish fashion shows in spectacular settings such as that held in Dunsany Castle in 1953.

PLATE 16 'Cossack' suit by Sybil Connolly, winter 1956. A striking day suit in which the fabric is a strong design element. *Courtesy* Harper's Bazaar/*The National Magazine Company (Photo: Richard Dormer)*

Sybil Connolly followed up her first successful showing in the US and Canada with many more, and became extremely well known – she was featured in *Life* magazine in August 1953; she was even given a police escort in Atlanta, and named Miss Submarine by the US Pacific Fleet! In 1955 she made her first visit to Australia where she was invited to show her collection by the Australian Consolidated Press. This too proved immensely successful both for herself and for Irish cloth manufacturers.

In 1957 Sybil Connolly parted company with 'Richard Alan' and set up her own fashion house at 71 Merrion Square which has been her home, showroom and workplace ever since. She describes it, with reason, as 'the house that linen built'. She has expanded her design work to include fabric designs for Brunschwig et Fils. One of her most successful fabric designs was that based on the court dress of the eighteenth-century writer and artist Mrs Mary Delany[4] (who was described by Edmund Burke as 'the woman of fashion of all ages'). She organized an enormously successful exhibition of the latter's famous paper mosaics of flowers, owned by the British Museum, at the Pierpoint Morgan Library in New York in 1976. Miss Connolly has great admiration for this remarkable woman, whose energy, artistic gifts and wide circle of powerful friends so resemble her own. She is also a design consultant for Tiffany's of New York and has been responsible for some of their most successful lines, including Tommy Daly's parian porcelain, ranges of Tipperary glass and Nicholas Mosse pottery. She is proud of her work in keeping traditional fabric and other crafts alive. Her three books, *Irish Hands*, dealing with Irish crafts, *In an Irish Garden*, which she co-authored, and *In an lrish House*, give a good indication of her range of interests. Indeed, a strong interest in interior design is a characteristic of almost every fashion designer I have spoken to. It seems to be an automatic extension of their interest in a personal environment.

Sybil Connolly's and Jack Clarke's success overshadowed that of other designers of the 1950s because they combined between them all the elements necessary for large-scale success in the fashion world. These included basic good design ability combined with original and timely ideas as regards fabric; a reliable, effective and well-funded manufacturing and workroom system which could efficiently produce both couture and top quality ready-to-wear; sound business sense which could identify and supply markets; a strong export drive and an extremely successful selling technique which relied on a strong and charming personality. This formula is still a recipe for success.

While Sybil Connolly raised the international profile of Irish fashion considerably, this new reputation was also sustained by the great talents of other designers whose work in many ways ran in parallel lines to that of Miss Connolly. The 'zeitgeist' of fashion was as evident in 1950s' Ireland as at any other time and place.

Irene Gilbert was one of the traditional perfectionist couturiers, widely respected by her peers, customers and staff. Cecily McMenamin, now fashion buyer at Brown Thomas, the fashion designer Pat Crowley,

PLATE 17 Day suit by Irene Gilbert, winter 1954, showing the effective use of obviously Irish fabric. Courtesy Harper's Bazaar/*The National Magazine Company (Photo: Richard Dormer)*

and Mrs Phyllis Seigne all worked for her in different capacities, and all bear witness to her skills in cutting and the quality of the hand finishing upon which she insisted. Working for her was hard but rewarding. She was, for over twenty years from the late 1940s until her retirement in 1968, a major and influential force in Irish fashion.

She studied fashion design in London after apprenticeship to a Dublin haberdasher, and returned to Dublin after the Second World

War. She opened her first shop in South Frederick Street in 1947, opened her salon in 1950, and showed her first collection in 1951. In 1958 she began showing her two collections per year in her own showrooms, at 117 St Stephen's Green from 1960. In 1954 she was sent by CTT with a collection to New York which gained an excellent press, followed by full British press coverage. She subsequently showed in England from 1955 onwards. Other work included costume design for film[5]. In 1957 she designed the Aer Lingus uniform, and did so again in 1966 using Magee's tweed and Moygashel linen.[6]

Like Madeleine Vionnet, the great French couturière, Irene Gilbert often designed directly on a stand. She saw the fashion potential of Irish fabrics, which became a dominant feature in her designs. She worked closely with mills to obtain richly coloured tweeds which were light enough even for dress use.

She was particularly associated with the Avoca Handweavers company. Her much-admired hydrangea coloured tweeds of 1955, for example, were the result of sending the Misses Wynn of Avoca a dried hydrangea head to indicate the colours she wanted. She also worked closely with Bill McNutt of Downings, Magees of Donegal, and other mills. Often she used one yarn from a tweed to crochet yokes, overblouses, etc. She also used linen to good effect. Although Miss Gilbert was associated with Irish natural fabrics, she also used English and continental fabrics and was not averse to experimentation with some of the new manmade fabrics such as lurex and acetate.

Irene Gilbert's impeccable tailoring was probably seen to best advantage in day wear, but her evening dresses were also remarkable, especially her handmade lace dresses and, in the 1960s, her draped dresses. Her patrons included Princess Grace of Monaco, for whom she made a Carrickmacross lace evening dress, Mrs Sean T. O'Kelly, for whom she designed outfits for her presidential visit to the United States, and Anne, Countess of Rosse.

The late Countess was one of the most outstanding patrons of fashion of her day, and her knowledge of the subject was enormous. She promoted Irish fashion most effectively, particularly when on working trips to the US, with the Earl of Rosse, who was then Vice Chancellor of Dublin University. She was one of Irene Gilbert's greatest admirers, and most loyal patrons, as can be seen from the impressive collection of Gilbert outfits at her Irish home, Birr Castle.[7]

Neilli Mulcahy was another Irish couturière who made most effective use of native materials, especially wool. She is one of several Irish designers who have said to me that the cloth always dictated the design. She worked with McNutts, Avoca, Molloys, Gaeltarra

PLATE 18 Evening dress by Irene Gilbert, 1954. One of her classic draped evening gowns, for which she was justly famous.
Courtesy Harper's Bazaar/*The National Magazine Company (Photo: Richard Dormer)*

'The cloth always dictated the design'

NEILLI MULCAHY

Eireann and other firms, and speaks nostalgically of their enthusiasm and willingness to produce short lengths. She also used poplin and linen a good deal. In the 1960s, printed woven or knitted wool was a notable feature of her work. The printing was done by Michael McInerney who worked at Liberty.

After a variety of courses, Neilli Mulcahy became one of the first of many subsequently well-known Irish designers to attend the Grafton Academy of Dress Designing, founded by Mrs Pauline Clotworthy. After other training jobs in Dublin she set off for Paris with her friend, the milliner Elizabeth Fanagan, and worked with Jacques Heim for some months. This experience of the best of couture standards was invaluable. (An extreme example of these standards, was the requirement that she sewed thirty-four buttons on to a dress at one sitting, lest her hand movement, and thus the finish of the work, altered.)

Neilli Mulcahy opened her own couture house in 1952 with a work-force of three, whom she trained herself. The company expanded, but

PLATE 19 HM Queen Elizabeth and the Earl and Countess of Rosse at Buckingham Palace, early 1950s. The Countess of Rosse is wearing an evening dress by Irene Gilbert, whom she often patronized. (Photo: Robert Graham)

PLATE 20 Tweed suit by Neilli Mulcahy, early 1960s. A good example of the classic tweed suit, with knitted section of the same tweed yarn. (Photo: Tony Higgins)

despite encouragement by CTT to go into factory production, it remained a made-to-measure establishment. Her products were helped by Sybil Connolly's success in the US and sold well there. Germany too was a good market where clients particularly liked the tweeds.

All the above couturiers took part in the large-scale fashion and trade shows put on by big trans-continental stores or by city fashion groups in the US, usually with the help of CTT. At many of these shows the Irish designers were in direct competition and appearing on the same catwalks as the most eminent Parisian couturiers. By all contemporary accounts they stood up well to the comparisons. All firms, no matter how well known they were in Europe, had to take the same steps to find their way to the lucrative markets and wealthy clients of America.

One of the most successful exporters was Donald Davies whose business was started in 1955. He originally came to Ireland to start up a branch of a London shirtmaking firm Knight and Petch. He was not a couturier but produced high-quality ready-to-wear garments mostly of light, beautifully coloured fine 'Crock of Gold' wools. The Farrell family who lived near the Davies home, 'Charleville', in Enniskerry, Co. Wicklow, wove shawls, and were asked by Donald Davies to make a firmer weave. When this was perfected he ordered 5,000 yards (4,572 metres) and set to producing shirts in his stables. He aimed for the American market from the start, partly because of tax incentives, and his marketing techniques were very successful. On his first trip to the States he won accounts all over the country starting with Lord and Taylor in New York. From the outset he never underestimated the importance of selling. His business sense was equalled by his wife Mary's sense of colour and design. Her bold, rich tweeds, checks and stripes gave the garments much of their distinction. Their casual, easy styles related to those of the American Claire McCardell whose comfortable and sporty designs dominated the high quality ready-to-wear US market.[8]

'Charleville' was a wonderfully impressive mansion which was factory, home and business centre. One happy result of this combination occurred when an American buyer who was entertained there was impressed with the school shirt of one of the Davies' sons. At her suggestion it was reproduced as the 'Paddy Shirt', and became a bestseller. Another development was the shirt dress which became a design classic, and was exported not only to the United States but to Europe and Japan in huge quantities. 'Charleville' was sold in 1978 and Donald Davies returned then to England, but the factory continued for many years.

Another designer/manufacturer who was one of the first to take advantage of the export market was Jimmy Hourihan, who started his company in 1955 which still survives. With CTT help and with the usual combination of luck and judgement he began to sell in the United States. A New York taxi driver, seeing his trademark Donegal tweed coats told him, 'You'll never sell those in this town, bud,' and sent him to the Ivy League University towns, where they sold very well. He also sold sucessfully very early in his career to high-quality outlets in England, such as Harrods. For some years before the Anglo-Irish Free Trade Agreement of 1965, however, he was forced to the expedient of a plant in Belfast where linings were sewn into his coats, since the use of any manmade fibre, even if it were only a label, in an Irish made garment made it liable to very heavy duty. Such were the difficulties of the pre-EU years.

PLATE 21 Checked wool dinner dress by Donald Davies, early 1960s. The strong contrasting colours – the bodice is dark blue, the skirt red and white – are typical of the designer's work.
Collection Ulster Museum

Jimmy Hourihan's reputation derives from the export of his Irish tweed coats and suits. As John McNutt commented, it was the Jimmy Hourihans, who bought pieces every season, rather than the high profile designers who might buy pieces every few years, who kept his firm going. He, like Jack Clarke, helped to enhance the perceived image of Irish tweed abroad which has stood the industry in good stead. Now, however, he uses other cloths much more than native fabrics.

Henry White, good friend of Jack Clarke, also began exporting from the late 1940s. He directed his efforts to the UK market. His firm, which was established in 1934, survives to the present day, and still prides itself on the quality of its tailoring.

The above designers were those whose businesses were so long lived or so successful that their name and influence became well established. There were many others who worked to a high standard, and enjoyed a healthy contemporary reputation, but whose influence was not so long-lived. Raymond Kenna was well known in Dublin for his tweeds which were often very brightly coloured. He combined red and black a good deal in his evening wear. Some of his extravagant ideas, such as his cream tweed wedding dress with scarlet veil in 1957, were not always appreciated by his contemporaries and sound more attuned to present fashion concepts. Elizabeth James of Cork was a well respected house which produced well-tailored day wear, also specializing in tweeds and evening wear. Maureen Evans' designs were predominantly traditional Irish in inspiration and she interpreted Aran knitwear effectively into contemporary styles. Her influence on the export market was very great through her gifted design work and her standardization of sizing and quality. She also worked with Digby Morton when he blended hand knitting with hand-woven *bainin* in a series of sports styles for the US market. Nicholas O'Dwyer for some years had a very high-quality manufacturing business in Dublin, and opened a shop in Suffolk Street. Una Tully's retail designs broke the mould – their decorative details and casual sportiness derived their inspiration from the US.

THE LONDON IRISH

Expatriate Irish designers were as important an element in Irish fashion in the fifties as in the 1980s and 1990s. In the 1950s they were predominantly in London. Most remained proud of their Irish roots even though they were entrenched in English society, and they all made effective use of Irish fabrics. It is remarkable that of the designers in the Incorporated Society of London Fashion Designers four, namely, Edward Molyneux, John Cavanagh, 'Michael' and Digby Morton, were born in Ireland or were of Irish stock.

The Incorporated Society of London Fashion Designers was set up in 1942 to promote British clothing exports, in the wake of a successful joint collection tour of South America by a group of designers in 1941. The eight original members included Digby Morton and Molyneux (the first chairman). Later members included 'Michael' and John Cavanagh. The original members helped promote the 'Utility' scheme of clothing resulting from the wartime need to restrict the amount of cloth in each garment. Their designs for mass production were very effective and economical and were sold from early 1943. The group members initiated and showed in London Fashion Week, held the week before the Paris shows, which for many years has successfully attracted world buyers.

Digby Morton was born in Dublin in 1906, and studied art and architecture in the Metropolitan School of Art, Dublin. He moved to London where he designed for the house of Lachasse, the first of three Irish designers to work there. This house became noted for its tailored suits, and he was responsible for the transformation of these severe garments into fashionable outfits. After he opened his own house in 1934 Morton's suits continued to be a successful feature of his collections, though his other day wear and evening wear were also very popular. He used softly coloured tweeds, often from Donegal, and was one of the first designers to use Aran knitwear as part of a high-fashion outfit. Apart from his Incorporated Society of London Fashion Designer work he designed uniforms and an off-the-peg range of clothes during the Second World War. Some of the most striking images of wartime fashion featured Morton's clothes, notably Cecil Beaton's 1941 photograph of fashion in the middle of bomb damage.

Right:
PLATE 22 Suit by Digby Morton, Vogue, *September 1941. Cecil Beaton's famous photograph of a sharply suited figure among bomb rubble was not just a fashion statement about the well-tailored suits which Digby Morton and other designers produced during the war years, but became a symbol of order amidst chaos. Cecil Beaton, ©* Vogue, *Condé Nast Publications Inc.*

After the war, Morton worked for US manufacturers in the mid-1950s and continued successfully with his own house until 1957. In 1958 he became director of the firm Reldon-Digby Morton. He was a gregarious man who 'rejoiced in his Irishness', as his friend, Felicity Green of the *Daily Telegraph*, remembers. Apparently he and his sister 'were a great Irish double act'. True to type, he was an inspired interior designer, who was 'a brilliant creator of houses' for himself and his journalist wife, Phyllis.

John Cavanagh was born in Ireland in 1914 and was brought up in England. He trained with Molyneux from 1932 until 1940, when he served in the Intelligence Corps. After the war he travelled in the USA, studying fashion promotion, and then worked with Pierre Balmain from 1947 until 1951. He opened his own house in 1952 and bravely took

PLATE 23 Jacket by John Cavanagh, 1956, showing the perfect finish of his elegant and refined designs. Courtesy of the Board of Trustees of the Victoria & Albert Museum (Photo: John French)

his complete collection to Paris in 1953. He soon had a large clientele, including many former customers of Molyneux, who had retired, including Princess Marina. He designed the wedding dresses of both the Duchess of Kent and Princess Alexandra, Princess Marina's daughter. His understated style has been compared to that of Molyneux, but he had his own distinctive simple elegance of line. In the 1960s he produced wholesale and ready-to-wear lines, and retired in 1974.

'Michael', Michael Donnellan was born in Ballinlough, County Roscommon in 1915. He studied medicine for five years at Trinity College Dublin before deciding on a change of direction. After the intervention of the Second World War and service in the RAF he studied at the British Fashion Institute for overseas students. His first post was as suit designer at Lachasse where he followed Digby Morton and Hardy Amies. In 1953 he opened his own couture house in Carlos Place, London. His understanding of the human body, superb tailoring and purity of line gave him a very high contemporary reputation, not least among his peers. He was often

'True elegance begins where fit ends'

MICHAEL

compared to his idol, Balenciaga, and in fact was invited to join Balenciaga's design team. The two men also shared a love of Chinese art of which they were both passionate collectors.

Hallmarks of the 'Michael of London' label were set-back, mostly bias-cut collars which framed the neck and head becomingly; sleeves finished level with the jacket hem (partly so that the widest part of the body, the hips, would not seem even wider); slightly dipped jacket backs; and short, curved waistbands with eased-in skirt fullness at the front and short skirt darts, to keep the hip shape rounded and apparently lengthen the legs. Skirts were always mounted panel by panel on to silk organza, so that hem stitching never showed and the skirts never seated. It is worth mentioning these details in order to give an idea of the standards of 1950s couture, which have not been bettered. They were given to me by Michael's great friend, the remarkable Leonora Curry. She was one of the first technical advisers to the clothing section of CTT, and has, over many years, contributed much to Irish fashion.

PLATE 24 Jacket made for the International Wool Secretariat by Michael, late 1950s. It shows his typical set-back collar, from which the neck and head emerge gracefully. Michael's work, which was of the highest couture quality, was greatly admired by his peers. International Wool Secretariat

In 1961 Michael was asked to become design consultant at Marks & Spencer, where he worked for two days a week. There he brought to High Street clothes of mass manufacture some of the standards and details of *haute couture*, upgrading cut and cloth. His legacy of short darts and narrow waistbands is still seen on Marks & Spencer's skirts. He also made ranges of clothes for American stores such as Bergdorf Goodman, Lord and Taylor and I Magnin.

Michael encouraged young talent, notably the milliner Graham Smith. Ib Jorgensen was given encouragement, too, when judged by him to be winner of the NIADA (National Industrial and Agricultural Development Association) fashion competition in Dublin in 1955. He maintained strong links with Ireland (as did Digby Morton), and did what he could to promote Irish fashion and Irish fabrics.

Michael closed his house in 1971, because of the lack of properly trained young people for his workrooms, without whom he could not maintain the standards he set himself. He was followed at Lachasse by another Irishman 'Owen of Lachasse', the Papal Count Michael MacSweeney who remained with the firm until the mid-1970s.[9]

MILLINERS

In the 1950s, accessories were a much more important part of the outfit than is now the case. At present, a hat or gloves may be worn either to enhance an outfit or for practical purposes, but may equally well be dispensed with. In the 1950s, however, and on into the early 1960s, they were an integral part of an outfit for formal outdoor day wear and for many specific social occasions. In the more formal world

PLATE 25 Portrait of Michael with his sketches, late 1940s. (Photo: Roland Haupt)

of the time, the laws of etiquette as well as custom and fashion enforced adherence to their use. Ireland produced many fine and well-trained hatters, who at that time could make a good living from made-to-measure work. Those whose work became used by and associated with couturiers won national and sometimes international reputations. John Green and Peta Swift worked for Sybil Connolly, Elizabeth Fanagan for Neilli Mulcahy, and Martyn Boswell, among others, for Irene Gilbert. Yvonne Modette of Dublin was also successful for many years. In London, Michael helped Graham Smith's career enormously through his patronage.

An account of the careers of two of these milliners, can serve to illustrate the successes and difficulties of the trade. John Green of Belfast trained at Paddington Technical College, and with Renée Pavy in London and Jean Barthet in Paris. He produced hats for Sybil Connolly's autumn/winter collection in 1955, and in spring/summer 1956 his 'hairdrier hat', which was seen in the press as pre-dating

PLATE 26 Straw hat by John Green, 1965. The strong shape and interesting texture are characteristic of John Green's designs. Collection Ulster Museum

Christian Dior's similar piece, received particular notice. Two hundred of his hats were sent with her outfits on her 1957 tour of Australia, and he continued to show with her periodically. He had his own salon in Wellington Street, Belfast from 1961. As demand for hats diminished from the mid-1960s he extended the range of merchandise and tried marketing ploys such as 'hat-tokens', miniature hats given to represent the hat which could be subsequently bought at leisure. His salon shut in 1975 and since then he has worked as an interior designer. John Green worked a good deal with Irish linen, and his fabric topstitching was a signature detail.

PLATE 27 Hat, c. 1964, by Elizabeth Fanagan, who used a wide variety of techniques and fabrics. (Photo: Robert Dawson)

Elizabeth Fanagan had been making hats for friends from an early age. She, like John Green, felt it necessary to leave Ireland for training, and also worked at Pavy's, before going to Jean Barthet in Paris and Bergdorf Goodman's workshops in New York. Her salon in Dublin was opened in 1962, and she enjoyed a wide clientele. She was particularly associated with Neilli Mulcahy, and also worked with Ib Jorgensen. She closed her salon in 1965, discouraged both by the decline of the hat trade and by the difficulty of finding new trained staff. Undeterred, she has enjoyed several occupations since then, and has taken a degree in social sciences.

CONCLUSION – USING IRELAND

Designers of the 1950s were highly aware that their Irishness was their great marketing strength. They used conspicuously Irish fabrics and very often the titles given to each model in a collection were rather laboured evocations of 'Celticism'. Examples taken at random include Irene Gilbert's 'Kilkenny Marble' and 'Irish Diamond', Sybil Connolly's 'Irish Washerwoman' and 'Bainin', Raymond Kenna's 'Strongbow' and 'Druid's Spell', Neilli Mulcahy's 'Stirabout' and 'Aer Lingus'. A fine line had to be drawn between taking Ireland and Irish fabrics as an initial inspiration and allowing the Irish connection to become mawkish and hackneyed. As early as 1955 journalists such as Caroline Mitchell of the *Irish Times* were warning of the dangers of 'lifting a Celtic design and planting it down piecemeal on a cocktail frock' rather than translating 'Irish' colours, fabrics and designs into impeccably stylish garments.

On the whole the fabric and fashion makers served each other well, particularly as far as the woollen weavers were concerned. An initial advantage was that fine tweeds and unusual weaves in wools were internationally fashionable. The new weights, colours and weaves which Irish weavers produced in response to the demands of fashion designers found welcome new markets at home and abroad. Sales of wool could go up by 100 per cent in dollar countries after marketing trips by designers. Finding an exclusive source of an original fabric became a preoccupation for Irish designers. Mostly they worked closely with long-established firms, such as those whose names have already appeared in this chapter. This was normally a fruitful collaboration which occasionally involved the weavers in the difficult position of having to hold back yardage of a particular weave until a collection was launched. Sometimes designers went to craftsmen/weavers such as Gerd Hay-Edie of County Down, who could produce very unusual weaves like the 'shaggy dog' cloth which Sybil Connolly used to great effect in 1956.[10] Sometimes, too, they used original and

'The greatest common link between the Paris, London and Dublin couturiers is – well, what do you think? Tweed!'

IRISH TIMES

traditional fabrics, such as *bainin*, flannel, or the Foxford serge used by Raymond Kenna in 1956, bought at source.

The embroidery and lace-making producers also won wide new markets, and had to rethink their products. This gave them a new lease of life, and in some cases ensured their survival. St Louis' Convent in Carrickmacross, for example, was greatly helped by the patronage of Irish couturiers.

The linen industry was helped by the fabric's widely publicized use by Irish designers. Sybil Connolly's pleated linen in particular became very well known. Linen was also extensively used by the other designers of the 1950s. It was heavily promoted, both commercially and privately – for instance, the woman MP for West Belfast wore only linen on official business. Nevertheless, this help and promotion could not compensate for the decline in the household use of linen.

If the fabric producers were helped by fashion designers, the reverse was also true. Designers were working with materials which gave them a distinctive identity in the world of international fashion. Irish cloth was likely to appeal to the American market for sentimental reasons but it was also attractive to the European market, and it was bought by the most sophisticated Parisian couturiers.

The main export thrust, however, was overwhelmingly westwards to North America. In 1952 for example, the release of *The Quiet Man* (John Ford's hugely successful and highly romantic film set in the West of Ireland), the inception of the Dollar Board and the creation of Sybil Connolly's 'Irish Washerwoman' outfit all took advantage of the attraction of this island to the North American continent. This attraction was a vital factor in the success of the Irish fashion designers of the 1950s.

'Your tweeds are subtle, they have got the feel of the hands.'

SHEILA MULLALLY to GERD HAY-EDIE

3 CHALLENGING TIMES: THE 1960S AND 1970S

By 1960 Ireland's economy had begun to improve, and there were many concomitant social changes. The economic plans of T.K. Whitaker, Secretary of the Department of Finance, which involved help to agriculture, and the attraction of foreign capital and companies to Ireland began to ease unemployment and the flow of emigration. Business and marketing became more professional and educational standards improved drastically. The setting up of Kilkenny Design Workshops in 1964 at the instigation of Coras Tráchtála revolutionized public awareness of design, and continues its essential work in raising standards of industrial and craft design in Ireland.[1] The advent of national television in 1962 and increasingly effective marketing by Bord Failte brought the world to Ireland, and Ireland to the world. Ireland was becoming more outward looking and international in attitude – just as the new tourist industry was extolling its pre-industrial and unchanging charms.

This interconnection of past and present still characterized the work of many of the designers and fabric producers of the 1960s, certainly for the early years of the decade. Both established and new designers continued to use Irish fabrics, but in new weights, blends and weaves, and in contemporary international styles. Weaving firms might use foreign wools (frequently Australian), or mix mohair or cashmere with Irish wools or use the latter alone to produce a variety of cloth, from 'gossamer' tweeds to the more traditional coat tweeds. Wools were also printed, a new development much used by Neilli Mulcahy.

The new 'easy-care' manmade fibres, such as nylon, Orlon and Terylene, had begun to reach Ireland in the 1950s. In the early years of the sixties they were being manufactured in Ireland and were heavily promoted. Since, initially, they were used mostly for mass-produced knitwear and underwear they were not seen as a threat to natural fibres at a high fashion level.

During the twenty years, 1960–80, fashion designers on the whole fell into one of four groups: those whose careers began in the 1950s or early 1960s and continued until about 1970; those whose careers began in the

PLATE 28 Portrait of Mrs Jacqueline Kennedy Onassis by Aaron Shikler, 1970. The portrait depicts the former First Lady wearing a pleated linen dress by Sybil Connolly.
White House Historical Association

sixties and continued for at least another 25 years; those whose careers started and stopped in the seventies; and those whose careers started in the seventies but came to fruition in the eighties and nineties. If this seems an awkward simplification it serves to make sense of what may seem something of an interim period between the high points of the 1950s, and 1980s and 1990s Irish fashion. As a transitional time between two very different eras, however, it had its own energy and creativity.

THE DESIGNERS

The Irish Tradition

The designers of the 1950s continued in business but with less international acclaim, as the 'shock of the new' had gradually evaporated. Sybil Connolly no longer showed in Dublin but concen-

PLATE 29 Woven tweed and knitted tweed yarn outfit with cape by Neilli Mulcahy, mid–late 1960s (Photo: Tony Higgins)

trated her design efforts in the United States. The patronage of her work by Mrs Jacqueline Kennedy, the wife of the President, helped her reputation in America enormously.[2] Irene Gilbert moved to her St Stephen's Green premises in 1960 and continued to show in Dublin, London and the USA. Neilli Mulcahy's business flourished, and Donald Davies continued to export to great effect.

New designers started successful businesses in the 1960s and some who had started in the 1950s came to prominence. The following five, initially at least, maintained a strong traditional Irish identity.

In 1964, Sheila Mullally opened her own business at her home in Wellington Road, Dublin. Previously she had designed for the Elizabeth James firm in Cork which had a good reputation for fine tailoring using Irish tweeds.[3] Sheila Mullally was one of many dress designers who originally had intended architecture as a career; some buyers commented on the fact that this was evident in her garments' construction. She spent the first years of her business building up her exports to the US and Canada. She was a tall woman and made generously cut clothes with a strong 'Irish look', a combination which appealed to the North American market. A striking feature of her work was its distinctive fabric, and she collaborated from 1961 with Gerd Hay-Edie of Rostrevor, who had produced some of Sybil Connolly's most successful fabric in the 1950s and in the sixties worked more and more with dress tweeds. Once Sheila had her own house her colour range became more and more vibrant. The two women often worked to a tight schedule so that the tweeds could not be copied by other weavers – the weave was a very important selling point of the garment.

PLATE 30 Evening dresss by Clodagh, 1962, which shows the successful and sophisticated use of a heavily textured fabric in a high fashion garment. (Photo: Alen MacWeeney)

Clodagh O'Kennedy, whose label was simply 'Clodagh', began her fashion career at the precocious age of seventeen in the 1950s after a course at the Grafton Academy. By the sixties she became increasingly influential in Irish fashion as a designer, journalist and boutique owner. She exported successfully to the US, particularly from the time she sold her collection to Lord and Taylor in 1963. She used a wide variety of wools, some extraordinarily fine, and collaborated with knitters, weavers, fabric painters and crochet makers. She was one of the first designers to integrate all elements of her fashion shows – clothes, music, movement, hair, make-up and accessories – into a totality which foreshadowed both future developments in presentations and her own future interior design career.

Throughout her life the wellspring of Mary O'Donnell's inspiration has been not only the fabric tradition but also the literary and artistic traditions of her country. She was born in Donegal, and was spinning and carding wool by the time she was thirteen. At sixteen she was

PLATE 31 Crochet dress by Mary O'Donnell, one of her many designs for the performing arts. (Photo: Frank Fennell)

apprenticed to a dressmaker cousin. In 1950 she went to New York, where after other work experience she spent two-and-a-half years at Mainbocher, then the premier couture house of the United States. After returning to Ireland, she worked with Sybil Connolly before starting her own house in 1963. The best of her garments have a great simplicity which is possibly Mainbocher's legacy, combined with interesting, often very textural, fabrics.

Many of Mary O'Donnell's later designs were theatrical, made for 'fashion ballets' or to be shown in combination with poetry recitations, most frequently the work of W.B. Yeats. This work is original, idiosyncratic and often exquisitely worked and embroidered. She also designed costume for film, for example for *The Summer of the Falcon* (1981) which was based on the story of Tristan and Isolde, whose mythical Celtic subject matter appealed to her design interests.

The work of Kay Petersen was also steeped in literary allusion. Her boutique in Dawson Street in Dublin was called 'Anna Livia', named for 'Anna Livia Plurabelle', the personification of the River Liffey ('only feminine river in Europe') on which Dublin stands, from James Joyce's *Finnegans Wake*. She is remembered, too, in Louis MacNeice's memoirs for her prominent and individual part in the 1962 'Bloomsday' celebrations.[4] Her design work was heavily reliant on Irish fabric, notably brilliantly coloured tweeds, for both day and evening wear. Her tailoring standards were high, partly thanks to Thomas Wolfangel who worked with her in the mid-1960s before opening his own house.

Pat Crowley was born in the west of Ireland, and she has often commented upon how the extraordinary quality of the light there shaped her early artistic sensibility. She trained and worked with Irene Gilbert for seven years, and frequently represented her in the US, when the Dollar Board sent out Irish designers to stores throughout America. She opened her own hand-knitting business in 1967. Her first collection which had a 'Celtic' theme was of Irish crochet tops, skirts and wedding dresses. In collaboration with McNutts of Donegal, she coordinated yarns for knitting and crochet with tweeds for skirts and trousers. Buyers from three big American stores bought from the Crowley collection, and photographers were sent over from the United States. This gave her good publicity and was a great boost to the business, but also underlined the difficulties of such a small operation where quick re-orders were very problematic – 'there was no way we could do it!' Gradually the knitwear gave way to the more lucrative wedding-dress business. Her couture range, which she designed from 1976, was sold in her Duke Street boutique, where she also stocked top European designers' work.

Right:
PLATE 32 Sketch of a costume based on W. B. Yeats' poem 'The Song of Wandering Aengus', by Mary O'Donnell, made for the Yeats Pageant of Poetry, Music and Dress which she created, 1978–80, for the Irish American Cultural Institute, in St Paul, Minnesota. It was hosted by HSH Princess Grace of Monaco.

In the early 1980s Pat Crowley won a new clientele of American socialites as a result of a very successful fashion show in New York in 1982, and her business there continues to flourish. She is perhaps most closely associated with the grand ballgown in couture tradition, but she has a sharp eye for changing trends and lifestyles. Her work in the 1990s for both day and evening is much more pared down and adaptable. An outfit by Pat 'brings you quite a distance' and is now geared to the requirements of women who need a compact travelling wardrobe. Pat has always used Irish fabric as well as European and continues to do so.

All the above designers had a strong Irish image, which to a greater or lesser extent they used as a marketing ploy. Most of them also

PLATE 33 Crochet dress, 1971, by Pat Crowley who was one of the first designers to produce fashionable, youthful and casual garments in crochet. (Photo: Tony Higgins)

produced work which had no intrinsic relationship to Ireland and was simply part of the international couture tradition, a trend which increased as the 1960s passed. Classic Irish couture, particularly evening wear, became a genre of its own, and by the mid to late 1960s ceased to be relevant to mainstream Western European fashion. It has to be said that at its best the style remains undeniably beautiful, as I was reminded when I recently saw a Pat Crowley Irish hand-crocheted bodice with a pale turquoise silk poplin skirt.

PLATE 34 Evening dress by Pat Crowley, 1990. A good example of the designer's grand but pretty and flattering evening outfits. (Photo: Tony Higgins)

The International Tradition

Not all of Ireland's fashion designers of the 1960s produced work which was quite so self-consciously Irish. Four designers whose long fashion careers only had occasional Irish references first came to notice during this decade. Three of these were not even Irish by birth.

The first of these, Ib Jorgensen, came to Ireland with his family from Denmark in 1949. He, like Sheila Mullally, had ambitions for an architectural career, but changed direction and studied dress design at the Grafton Academy. Ib worked briefly on his own but then spent three invaluable years working for Nicholas O'Dwyer's clothing company. The finishing standards of his elderly workforce, inherited from an old Jewish tailoring business, left an enduring legacy. Jorgensen finishing has always been of very high quality, and his tailoring, too, seen best in day wear, is of the highest standard.

Ib Jorgensen opened his own house in 1958, initially on a small scale, but with increasing success in the 1960s. His business was at a peak in the seventies, when he had splendid showrooms and a home in Fitzwilliam Square and a boutique in Dawson Street. He exported to the United States, but mostly to London; Liberty was one important customer and for some years he had a shop in Bond Street. He had a large private clientele in Ireland, England, and the US.

Ib used Irish tweeds and linen in day wear, and Irish poplins and Carrickmacross lace in his tailored cocktail and evening wear. Irish motifs were sometimes used in the printed, hand-painted and embroidered designs of his first wife Patricia Jorgensen in the 1970s which were another striking hallmark of the house. His essential image, however, was of high quality, classic, international design.

For many years Ib Jorgensen collaborated with another foreign designer, Michelina Stacpoole, who made Ireland her home. She was born in Italy and trained there at a couture house and then with Krizia in Rome. She came to Ireland to learn English and decided that she wanted to stay. After a variety of jobs she set up Hollypark Knitwear with Mrs Heather Cohane in 1966. This business, which started with

PLATE 35 Evening dress of fine cotton by Ib Jorgensen, hand painted by Patricia Jorgensen. The 1970s design collaboration between Ib and Patricia Jorgensen, mostly involving the painted and embroidered embellishment of evening wear, produced some of the most striking designs of the house.
(Photo: Tony Higgins)

only one machine, became very successful. In 1972 she left Hollypark and set up her own factory at her home at Pallaskenry, County Limerick. It has 8-gauge hand-loom Dubied machines at which her staff of five, using 100 per cent wool from France, make sophisticated knitwear, with not a cable in sight. Her work has changed radically, with fashion, over the years. It was soft, fitting and tweedy in the 1970s and chunky and layered then business-like in the eighties, and now, in the nineties, is pared down and simple. 'Trendy is short-lived, style is forever', is one of her dictats, though it loses some of its effect when not heard spoken in a forceful Italian accent. The designers she would most comfortably be compared with are the late Jean Muir of the UK and

Sonia Rykiel of France. She sells in Dublin, and also, in an unusual but successful combination with her husband, George Stacpoole, the well-known antique dealer, in his shop in Adare, County Limerick.

Richard Lewis began his fashion career in 1965, after a course at the Grafton Academy. His family background was in clothing, producing school uniforms and nuns' habits, and at an early age he determined to have his own business. Initially, he worked as a freelance designer and as a manufacturer, before establishing his own couture house, where he could design for individuals.

Richard Lewis has, for many years, with his business manager, Jim Greevy, run a small salon, workshop and staff, thus avoiding crippling

PLATE 36 Cape and trousers by Ib Jorgensen, with co-ordinated knitwear by Michelina Stacpoole, early 1970s. International Wool Secretariat

PLATE 38 Jacket by Richard Lewis, 1981. Although best known for his designs in jersey, Richard Lewis's tailoring skills, as seen here, are equally impressive. (Photo: Breffni Ryan)

overheads. He makes to order, and also for a few ready-to-wear outlets in Ireland, the UK and the US. Apart from a brief foray into mass retailing with A-Wear in the early 1990s he has not sought to expand overmuch. Over the years Richard has created his own individual and respected niche in Irish fashion. He is probably best known for his fluid use of matt jersey, also wool crêpe and crêpe de Chine, in beautifully coloured draped outfits. He cannot simply be called the Irish Jean Muir[5] or Madame Grès,[6] however, for his sharply tailored garments are another strong element in his work, which is often referential to the 1930s and '40s. Another year's inspiration was the 'priest dress' look of

Left:
PLATE 37 Knitted outfit by Michelina Stacpoole, 1976. Her work is in the European tradition, and is almost completely non-referential to her adopted country. (Photo: Tony Higgins)

PLATE 39 Coat, autumn/winter 1983, by Thomas Wolfangel, whose strongly tailored coats and suits are his most successful ranges. (Photo: Tony Higgins)

1992 (accessorized with crucifixes a year before they were *the* Western European fashion accessory).

Thomas Wolfangel came to Ireland from his native Stuttgart, in Germany, in 1957. He first worked in Sligo before moving to Dublin where he opened his own business in the mid-1960s. By training as a tailor, his strength has always been his day suits, which are often in sharp, bright colours and which often include his characteristic sleeve detail and pin tucking. He diversified his couture business by opening a boutique in Lower Baggot Street in 1978. The buyer for the boutique was Kay Petersen, with whom Thomas Wolfangel had worked in the 1960s. Both were firm advocates of a revival of the use of strongly coloured Irish tweeds. Now he uses Irish tweeds only when the price is right, but they often still form his bestsellers.

Thomas Wolfangel uses some factory production for export wear and to supply his west of Ireland retail outlet, but most of his production is made-to-measure, at prices which compare very favourably with top of the range ready-to-wear. This is only possible because he and his workforce of six to eight can work extremely quickly to a very high level of skill. Dressmaking is still a craft to him and one which he sees threatened by a lack of positive encouragement by the State.

CHANGES IN THE WORLD OF FASHION

The late 1960s were difficult years for the established international fashion world, and these difficulties had their local manifestations in Ireland, overlaid with the country's own growing economic problems.

The youth culture of the middle to late 1960s, centred in London, occurred at a time of economic growth and high employment. The post-war baby-boom generation, the first young adults to enjoy free third-level education in the UK, had disposable income which was often spent on their appearance. In the fifties most teenagers had looked much like their parents, and peer group dressing was largely confined to 'teddy-boys' and 'beatniks'. By the sixties teenagers and post-teenagers as a generation dressed in a conspicuously different way from their parents, in outfits by new young designers. The cost of fabric was much reduced, due to the use of manmade fibres which were now used in high fashion garments, and shapes were simple, which much reduced labour costs. Clothes, therefore, became for the first time cheap enough to be, if not disposable, at least readily renewable, and fun. The designers with most impact were not the Parisian couturiers but the young London designers, most notably Mary Quant and, a little later, 'Biba', Barbara Hulanicki.

'Haute couture cannot be modernized'

YVES SAINT LAURENT[7]

The Parisian couturiers found themselves wrong-footed for once. They could certainly produce youthful styles, but the standards of made-to-measure *haute couture* were, for 'fun' dresses, inappropriate. Yves St Laurent was, as so often, right in his response to this problem, and produced, first for men and then for women, a *prêt-a-porter* range. He also diversified into franchising and helped develop the now almost standard system by which the essentially loss-making made-to-measure garments, as seen in the catwalk shows, create the image which sells the money-making perfume, make-up, hosiery, etc. He also had strong financial backing and a shrewd financial adviser, vital attributes for a successful designer.

In Ireland, too, social and economic changes posed difficulties for both made-to-measure couturiers and ready-to-wear designers. Although the national growth rate was still high, Ireland's economy still relied very heavily on foreign capital and investment and borrowing and unemployment were also high. Wage costs rose sharply in the 1960s and would spiral in the 1970s. Traditionally wages in the clothing trade had been low, even for expert hands, to the advantage of the business in the fifties. The combination of these higher costs and the reduced demand for high quality, expensive clothing made many choose to cut their losses and abandon their businesses at about this time. A sense that their world was changing and that they were out of tune with youthful, casual and cheap international fashion also helped persuade some couturiers to quit. Neilli Mulcahy for example, who retired in 1970, could see that changes in the tweed industry, which meant that women could go into a store and see a rack of perfectly good tweed skirts, also meant that her made-to-measure business was bound to diminish. Irene Gilbert retired in 1968 and Clodagh left Ireland for Spain in 1972, and thereafter pursued a career in architectural design. She moved to New York seven years later.[8]

Jack Clarke shut his factory in 1972, retaining 'Richard Alan' as a retail shop. He was an enormously influential and respected figure in Irish fashion design and manufacture. A perfectionist, his remarkably well-made clothes had fitted a niche somewhere between couture and ready-to-wear. However, as his son Richard Clarke said, he increasingly found that his price range no longer fitted new US market expectations. Even by trying to produce a cheaper range he could not compete in the US market. His prices, to be economical, had to rise to a level where volume of sales fell. Many other similar manufacturing firms were also forced to close at about this time. Although exports of ready-to-wear clothing became more and more difficult, exports of knitwear continued to increase, but these were not yet, on the whole, at the level of high fashion.

As the 1970s advanced, the situation in Ireland, economically and politically, became ever more grim. The intensification of violence in the north of Ireland, and the harsh realities of the energy crisis, inflation, recession and increased unemployment, made the relatively prosperous 1960s seem like a golden age. Old established businesses continued to fail and as shopping patterns changed many long-established department stores began to close. For years they had provided the general public with its most readily accessible view of the world of fashion.[9] Fledgling businesses, too, frequently folded once the years of financial help were past. Not only were many previously successful ventures no longer

PLATE 40 Knitted wool outfit, early 1970s, by Bill Gibb, who with his friend and collaborator Kaffe Fassett was one of the trailblazers in the 1970s development of knitwear as high fashion, which had such impact on the Irish knitwear industry. Collection Ulster Museum

financially viable because of wage costs but their markets were flooded with goods made for much less in the Third World.

Fortunately, international fashion, in reaction to the materialistic, plastic 1960s, and in tune with the very new concern for and interest in the conservation of the planet and its resources, began to drift in directions which again were advantageous to the innate qualities of Irish fashion. Two developments in particular laid the foundations of the great successes of the 1980s: the move back to natural fibres, and the new high fashion profile of knitwear.

The fashionable return to natural fibres began as the linen industry's prospects seemed very dismal. New technology in spinning, weaving and finishing had been adopted, however, and it was realized that marketing and design would have to improve, and restructuring would be necessary, if Irish linen was to regain international markets. The industry was therefore prepared for, and able to benefit from, the revival of linen as a fashion fabric which occurred in the late 1970s and '80s. The wool industry in Ireland was not under such ominous threat as the linen industry, although synthetic fibres had made inroads into its market too. It had already adapted its production methods to a wide variety of specialist yarns and weaves.

The elevation of knitwear to high fashion had its first manifestation in the work of Bill Gibb, Kaffe Fassett and Patricia Roberts in London, and Kenzo and Joseph in the early 1970s in Paris. Both body-hugging and thick-layered shapes were fashionable. Vivid colours in striking patterns were often employed which helped to lessen knitwear's hitherto rather staid and conservative image.

Ireland already had a very healthy export market for knitwear, an existing system of production, as evidenced by a thriving cottage industry, and a body of talented young designers who already were experimenting with new shapes. Even more crucially, there existed a creative vocabulary of pattern. The explosion of talent in and success of 1980s Irish knitwear had its roots in the '70s, both in the work of designers who began long successful careers then, and also, it must be said, in the work of the many talented designers whose careers, through ill luck, ill management, the prevailing economic conditions or choice, did not outlast the decade.

Examples of these were Betty Nolan, who ran an export and domestic crochet business in Roundwood, Co. Wicklow, using new designs and fresh colours, and the multi-talented Agnes Bernelle who developed knitting stitches which made beautiful evening dresses at Castle Leslie, Co. Monaghan. Both for some years ran successful businesses. The most remarkable of the knitwear firms which began in the 1970s, and which still flourishes, is probably 'Inis Meain Knitwear', run by Tarlach de Blacam, which will feature in the next chapter. Cyril Cullen's knitwear company also started in the mid-seventies and continues to thrive.

Cyril Cullen was a civil servant who had learned how to knit for a bet and continued to do so as a hobby. Only when he accepted a large number of knitwear commissions from Adele Astaire's house guests at Lismore Castle in the early 1970s and he was forced to find knitters and premises for his orders, did he give up his former career. He

PLATE 1 An Irish Woman c. 1700, Anon, watercolour.
An example of the red gown or petticoat with green apron and jacket, worn in the late seventeenth and early eighteenth centuries in Ireland, which has spawned so many 'Irish' dolls' costumes. The red petticoat which was at one time common wear throughout much of Europe, survived until the twentieth century in Ireland.
By permission of The British Library

PLATE 2 Cardigan, red skirt, apron, knitted shawl, headscarf and pampooties (raw hide shoes), all from the Aran Islands, early twentieth century. © National Museum of Ireland

PLATE 3 Evening dress, 1953, by Sybil Connolly. This romantic image typifies evening wear of the 1950s. The flattering proportions of dresses like this have made them 'design classics' which still inspire the styles of grand ball gowns today. Courtesy Harper's Bazaar*/The National Magazine Company. (Photo: Richard Dormer)*

PLATE 4 Checked wool day dress by Donald Davies, 1964. The use of bold checks in the dress fabric was a perennial feature of Donald Davies' designs. Originally published in the Telegraph Weekend Magazine *1964. (Photo: Terence Donovan)*

PLATE 5 Evening outfit by Ib Jorgensen, embroidery design by Patricia Jorgensen, mid-1970s. A good example of the Jorgensens' collaborative work in the 1970s. (Photo: Tony Higgins)

PLATE 6 Draped jersey outfit by Richard Lewis, 1989, showing his skilful working of this fabric, and his sure use of colour. (Photo: Breffni Ryan)

PLATE 7 Sinead O'Connor modelling for John Rocha at his first Paris show in 1994. Painted dresses were a strong feature of this collection. He was the first Irish designer to show in Paris since John Cavanagh in 1953. (Photo: Niall McInerney)

PLATE 8 Outfit from John Rocha's autumn/winter 1995 menswear collection, modelled by Bob Geldof. John Rocha first produced menswear in 1991, and it has become a strong and original element of his design work. (Photo: Niall McInerney)

PLATE 9 Country pursuits. Left, jacket, shirt, cravat, jodhpurs and waistcoat by Michael Mortell; right, jacket by Jonathan Richards, trousers by Gerrard, waistcoat by John Molloy, sweater by Castle of Ireland, shirt by Club Tricot, both caps by Hats of Ireland. An Bord Tráchtála/The Irish Trade Board

PLATE 10 Catwalk shot of Paul Costelloe's autumn/winter 1994 collection, which shows his loose, easy style. (Photo: Robert Fairer)

PLATE 11 The Princess of Wales wearing a short evening dress by Bellville Sassoon-Lorcan Mullany.
Copyright © Express Newspapers

PLATE 13 Day outfit autumn/winter 1993 by Peter O'Brien, designer for 'Rochas', showing clever use of strongly patterned wool fabric by Tim Roberts, who works from Newtownards, Co. Down. (Photo: Pascal Therme)

PLATE 12 *Jacket by Edel McBride, showing the North American inspired 'denim' knitwear which was typical of her work of 1993. (Photo: Chris Neely)*

PLATE 14 A striking photograph of an outfit by Glynis Robins which echoes the romantic image of her designs, 1993. (Photo: Lois Crighton)

PLATE 15 Part of a fashion spread, 1993, showing an outfit by Ann Demeulemeester, styled by Isabella Stanhope and modelled by Helena Christensen, which reveals rural Ireland for once as far from idyllic. Courtesy ELLE (UK) (Photo: Perry Ogden)

PLATE 16 Knitted outfit by Lyn-Mar (Lynn Elliott), 1995, which demonstrates her distinctive use of yarn. (Photo: Barry McCall) IMAGE Magazine October 1995

PLATE 17 Suit by Michelle O'Doherty, 1996, showing her easy and accomplished tailoring. (Photo: Jim Crone)

converted an eighteenth-century house in Carrick-on-Shannon to be a home, studio and workshop and both lived and worked there until his recent move to a castle in County Tipperary. Cyril Cullen's designs of the 1970s, although rooted in the Irish tradition, were typically vividly coloured with patchwork effect – quite a change from his present work which uses natural coloured Jacob sheep wool.[10]

By the 1970s, the infrastructure of the fashion world had changed quite radically from that of the 1950s and '60s. The decline of the demand for millinery spelt the rise in importance of the hairdresser. Hairstyles now had to complement the proportions and look of an outfit in the same way that had formerly been achieved by the hat. David Marshall of Dublin, who opened his salon in the mid-seventies was one of the new breed of hairstylists, much sought after for fashion shows and shoots. Stylists, make-up artists, and photographers together created a much wider variety of images than those seen in the essentially classic or romantic 1950s and '60s photographs. Fashion shows were becoming increasingly professionally choreographed, 'themed' with dance, music and effects. Models were careerists, not amateurs or girls filling in a few years before marriage.[11] The designers, too, were becoming more actively conscious of the need to market themselves effectively and formed the Society of Designers in Ireland (see Appendix 3).

The list of contributors to one of their fashion shows in 1977 gives a good overall picture of the couturiers, designers and designer/ manufacturers, old hands and newcomers who comprised the Irish fashion world. Almost all of these are still in business.

Sybil Connolly was in the show, as were Mary O'Donnell and Maureen Evans, all of whom were using primarily Irish materials, mostly working to an American taste and clientele. Ib Jorgensen who was the first chairman of the society also featured, as did Michelina Stacpoole, Pat Crowley, Jimmy Hourihan and Cyril Cullen.

Michael Jacobs was also in the show. His designer was Peter Fitzsimons, who was especially renowned for his well-tailored suit designs. Firms such as this very often took on the most talented of the new young graduates of the fashion courses. Yvonne Mahood, for example, was employed by Michel Ambers, and Enda Collier by Michael Gall. Award-winning graduate designers of the late 1970s and early '80s, like Patricia Keilthy, Liz Spillane, Liz Clery, Janice Smyth, Jacqui Smyth or Lorraine Egan who aspired to working with their own labels, very often went on to work for established companies, as the economic difficulties of the time made such independent operations more and more problematic and insecure.

Of the newly established young designers in this show, Paul Costelloe was to be by far the most successful. By 1977 he had already begun to make his name and had a shop in Drury Lane, Dublin. He had also already begun to use the Donegal tweeds and wools which became his trademark. He was born into the clothing business – his father was the manufacturer of the then famous Valstar raincoats. He trained in Ireland, at the Grafton Academy, and in France, at the Chambre Syndicale in Paris, where he studied design. This was followed by a couple of years working for Jacques Esterel and another two years designing in Milan. Before Paul returned to

PLATE 41 Hooded dress, late 1970s, by Cyril Cullen, one of the first generation of fashion knitwear designers in Ireland. An Bord Tráchtála/The Irish Trade Board

Ireland he went to the United States, his mother's country, and worked for a short time with Anne Fogerty. In 1979 he began his long and successful partnership with Robert Eitel, a Northern Irish business man, and with him set up the manufacture of his own label in the Strelitz factory in Moygashel, Dungannon.

Several other influential designers of the 1980s and '90s began their careers in the '70s. Carolyn Donnelly began her shop 'Ritzy' off Harcourt Street in 1978, making cheap, fun, party clothes. Liz Quin joined her in partnership and when 'Ritzy Design Studios' opened in Trinity Street, Dublin, it gave the first indication of the success of the Quin & Donnelly label. Mariad Whisker, from the north of Ireland, started her business in the mid-1970s and John Rocha and Eily Doolan began their designing careers in the late '70s in Kilkenny. The work and careers of all these will be dealt with in more detail in the next chapter on the 1980s, when their names became much more established, and when Irish fashion again took its place on the world stage.

4 HARD-WON GROUND: THE 1980S

BACKGROUND AND FASHION TRENDS

The 1980s was the decade when Irish fashion once more became a feature rather than a curiosity on the international fashion scene. Sadly, critical success was seldom synonymous with commercial success for the designers. They endured continuing recession in Ireland as well as the universal difficulties of fashion designers lacking strong financial backing, either private or governmental. The fact that most survived the decade alone is worthy of note.

Fashion is a response to the world and its economic, technical, cultural and aesthetic developments. It is multi-layered and ever-changing. Typically, the most striking and revolutionary elements which initially engage the interest quickly become hackneyed and exaggerated so that there sets in an equally strong reaction against them. Less strident features evolve more slowly, and if the proportion of the outfit remains pleasing, can last for many years. The 1980s saw a succession of different looks, both revolutionary and evolutionary. Sometimes styles spread quickly from country to country, and sometimes a strong look in one country barely reached, let alone survived, in another. For example, the elevation of the late 1970s, early 1980s street-style punk to a high-fashion statement which was particularly successful in London did not have an equivalent effect on Irish fashion. This was despite the fact that Irish bands made a strong contribution to the punk movement. However, Ireland has never, as the fashion historian and journalist Jane Mulvagh has pointed out, greatly favoured the urban club scene fashions which have for decades been such a distinctive feature of many young English designers' work.

The next major new development of the decade in international fashion did have a profound effect on Irish fashion. The Japanese designers' invasion of Paris of 1982 gave Western European fashion the same sort of shock that London's young designers had in the sixties. The Japanese garment's relationship to the human body was completely different to that of the tailored, body-hugging European garment. The oriental designs were often based on traditional Japanese work-wear, originally of linen or cotton. The fabric in its natural state, not stiffened, faced, or treated, dictated the often complex form of the garment which depended for effect on its fall, drape and texture. The proportion might be asymmetrical and change somewhat with each wearing as the garment fell over the body, but it was worked out with discipline and refinement. The mutual fascination and respect by European and Japanese designers for each other gave rise to a very healthy cross-fertilization of ideas. Japanese design, although initially seeming revolutionary to European designers, has become an example of the classic, evolutionary styles to which I have just referred, and it continues to wield a strong influence, particularly on knitwear designs.

The Japanese taste for untreated natural fabric together with their new concepts of construction diminished the importance of the creasing problems which had formerly so militated against the use of linen. This further helped the revival of linen as a fashion fabric. The Italians had begun to adapt cotton-spinning machines to linen in the 1970s, and Italian designers had already begun to use linen by 1975. Between 1979 and 1981 consumption of linen in the clothing sector in Europe rose fourfold. In Ireland the twenty or so linen weaving firms left of the two hundred in the early twentieth century took advantage of this trend. The Industrial Development Board of Northern Ireland, set up in 1982, urged the diversification of linen production to extend more to fashion wear, and new machinery and investment enabled the Irish producers to build up a share of the market which was dominated by the giant Italian textile firms. Enterprising firms such as Emblem Weavers of Wexford, run by Jim Conway, a former woollen weaver, and John England and others in the North brought new colours and weaves on to the market.

Irish designers of the early 1980s used Irish linen in new ways which directly or indirectly acknowledged the influence of Japan. Mariad Whisker used linen in a very individual way in her simple, beautifully proportioned outfits which often had a puritan feel. Their refinement and subtle colouring had something in common with Japanese designs. Paul Costelloe made light, unstructured linen suits. Michael Mortell quickly assimilated Japanese design and gave it his own stamp. His linen suit in the collection of the Ulster Museum in this Japanese/Irish style has a very complex and interesting cut. His subsequent designs in other fabrics, even manmade, continued to use elements of this style (see plate 42).

'Irish Linen inspired me more than any other fabric.'

MARIAD WHISKER

The new demand for Irish linen both at home and abroad was echoed by an increased demand for Irish wool, inspired by the same revival of taste for natural fibres. Irish designers and Irish fabric producers normally work in parallel, each serving the other from time to time.

PLATE 42 Linen suit by Michael Mortell, spring/summer 1985. The complex cut of this suit is a good example of Michael Mortell's skill in working with difficult or unusual fabrics.
Collection Ulster Museum
Model: Shannon, Style Academy

PLATE 43 Detail of outfit by Paul Costelloe, autumn/winter 1984. The successful blending of differently textured Irish fabrics is one of the strengths of this outfit.
Collection Ulster Museum

Occasionally, the lines converge when the Irish designer chooses to use predominantly Irish fabric. If the timing is right as far as the international market is concerned, it is often at these periods that the nationally known designer acquires an international reputation. It happened to Sybil Connolly in the 1950s, and to Paul Costelloe, particularly after his 1984 autumn/winter collection. His collection of Donegal herringbone tweed, crisp Irish linen shirts and Aran inspired knitwear gave him a high international profile which he has since retained.

As the 1980s advanced, the inevitable reaction to the shrouded body of the Japanese style had its most extreme advocate in the body-hugging work of designers such as Azzedine Alaïa,[1] who took the characteristics of exercise wear to high fashion. New, highly elastic and strong fibres, notably Lycra, which could be combined with natural fibres made this development possible. These styles pandered to the delusory notion of the aerobics generation that any body could be made to conform to an ideal form. Be that as it may, the highly body conscious clothes developed into 'power dressing' (the uniform of the female executive or would-be executive in what was formerly a man's world), most typically sharply tailored, short-skirted, fitted suits with ever more exaggerated shoulder lines.[2]

This type of sharp tailoring was readily produced by couturiers such as Thomas Wolfangel and Ib Jorgensen, designers such as Paul Costelloe, and manufacturers such as Dorene, Michael Jacobs and others. On the whole, however, they all tended to slightly soften the hard contemporary look.

Irish designers who were neither working to a mass market nor for made-to-measure customers were even more inclined to soften and romanticize this image. Designers such as John Rocha, in his 'Chinatown' range, and Michael Mortell produced very successful and individual collections with eighteenth- or nineteenth-century references in the late 1980s. These were more in tune with the work of influential new and more romantic designers such as Romeo Gigli,[3] whose rich, soft, wrapped designs led the reaction against the shoulder padded power dressing. John Rocha's great success of the late 1980s and '90s is an individual development of this simplified, gentle style of subtle proportion and texture, which again has reference to an Eastern inspiration.

As another alternative to the sharp, bright, impersonal power dressing, Irish designers adopted and developed the unstructured tailoring of the Italian Giorgio Armani,[4] who built a fashion empire on his fluid, soft-coloured, loosely fitting garments. Paul Costelloe often used Irish fabrics to give the look his distinctive touch. Louise Kennedy and Michelle O'Doherty have also developed this look in individual ways.

DESIGNERS

Designers of Clothes – In Ireland

Of all the Irish designers who came to prominence in the 1980s John Rocha has the greatest international reputation. Although he was raised in Hong Kong, with a Portuguese Catholic father and a Chinese Buddhist mother, he is claimed as an Irish designer because he has, since 1977, lived and worked in Ireland. He went to London in 1970, and became a psychiatric nurse for three years ('Very useful training for fashion business' as he said) before going to Croydon College of Design and Technology. He came to Ireland first with his future wife Eily Doolan and was inspired both by Irish fabrics, and also by a Mrs Mary Moylan who taught him much about lace, embroidery and crochet, and who still works for his collections. His final-year college show had a strong Irish theme, and CTT subsequently invited him to Ireland. It gave him a grant, and the business he and his wife set up in Kilkenny flourished. Softly tailored dresses, boxy jackets, often with oriental influence, and knitwear were typical of designs at this time. They moved to Dublin and although orders came in and new shops were opened in Dublin and Cork, the business failed due to lack of capital and cash-flow difficulty in the early 1980s. At the same time his marriage ended.

A new start came with a new company called Chinatown. He met Odette Gleeson who became his second wife, and an important member of his work team, not least because of her comments on the practicality of John's designs. She ran the Chinatown shop in Powerscourt Townhouse Centre in Dublin. This was the time of the romantic, almost historical versions of the sharply tailored styles then in vogue. Once again, however, despite popular success, business ran foul of the perennial and universal designer problems – basically the time lag between outlay of money on fabrics, etc, and the payment for garments from retailers. The shop closed in 1987.

The Rocha family moved to Milan for two years where John worked successfully for the manufacturer 'Reflections' under his own label. In 1989 he returned to Ireland to develop the 'Chinatown' by John Rocha concept, and from 1990 to 1994 he worked under licence to the Brown Thomas A-Wear group, where Deirdre Kelly, then fashion director of A-Wear, was keen to promote 'designer clothes at affordable prices'.

John Rocha's new headquarters in Temple Bar are a reflection of his status as an international designer whose business sells to twenty-eight countries – 70 per cent of his estimated £5 million turnover comes from overseas sales. Rocha's designs, during the third and most successful phase of his career, have become softer, simpler and more subtle. At their best the proportions of his garments are exquisite. His designs combine oriental shape and Celtic embellishment, Irish fabric and inter-national style. His day-wear tailoring is still strong, but more unstructured than during the 1980s. His evening wear is extraordinary – sheer rich fabrics in plain, effective shapes, often using hand-painted or printed designs by artists such as Clea van der Grijn or Lou Brennan. He also uses the skills of jewellers such as Slim Barrett to complement his work.

Highlights of John Rocha's recent career have been his winning of British Designer of the Year title in October 1993, which did much to establish his international name. His designs of that year, neutral, natural outfits with cropped tops and flamboyantly printed shift dresses both fitted current expectations and made an individual statement. A year later he showed in Paris for the first time – the first Irish designer to do so since Edward Molyneux and John Cavanagh.

PLATE 44 Suit, 1985, by John Rocha, a good example of the romantic, historically inspired and more softly tailored look which he and other Irish designers presented as an alternative to 1980s power dressing.
(Photo: Mike Bunn) IMAGE Magazine September 1985

His painted evening wear was the dominant feature of this show. The collection was well received in Paris, and became a cultural event of national importance in Ireland, filmed by Jim Sheridan.

Rocha still produces a knitwear range made by Hackett and Turpin in a former lace-making school in Belmullet and since 1991 has also produced menswear ranges. His new range of menswear is a brightly coloured departure from his usual colour range but still uses linens as well as a mixture of other fabrics.

John Rocha remains loyal to the fabrics and finishes of Ireland and

to the country itself. It is one of the anomalies of Irish fashion that a Portuguese-Chinese man from Hong Kong is perceived as an essentially Irish designer even as he wins a British Designer award. John Rocha can be seen perhaps as the Jack Charlton of Irish fashion – an obvious outsider whom all of Ireland considers as one of their own – a comparison which might please the designer, who is also a football fanatic.

Every design sphere has a 'designers' designer', one whom peers see as supremely skilled and innovative, and whom they admire without reservation. This figure usually has great design integrity, and more often than not is, comparatively speaking, a commercial failure, unless lucky enough to have sound business backing and advice. Michael Mortell is, in Ireland, the fashion designer whom many others will mention if asked which of their own number they most admire. (It must be noted, incidentally, that perhaps contrary to public expectation, Irish fashion designers are a most generous spirited and mutually supportive group of people. Generous praise for others is typical).

Michael Mortell comes from Cork, and trained in Belfast, London and Manchester, before working with Ib Jorgensen for two years. In 1978 he started his own label and began to produce the raincoats with which he has been associated ever since. He brought such flair to these seemingly unfashionable garments that they became, to borrow the awful consumer phrase, 'must-haves'. His skills were by no means limited to these garments however, as the host of awards he won in the early eighties can verify. These included three *Late Late Show* Designer of the Year awards and International Wool Secretariat awards. His eye and inspiration is international and eclectic and he has felt some sense of isolation in Ireland. He was, for example, as has been mentioned, quick to absorb and reinterpret the early eighties influence of Japanese designers. Other sources of inspiration have been the Hollywood-inspired styles as worn by Joan Crawford and Katherine Hepburn; the early twentieth-century Joycean period, and, the Irish country look, using, for example, McNutt tweeds and Aran sweaters. He makes all of these styles his own. His tailoring can be hard edge or soft, and his fabric use ranges from homespun to velvets to the latest micra fibres. Some commercial mistakes have come from 'peaking too soon', for example using waxed cotton three years before it became widely accepted.

Michael Mortell had a wide range of retail outlets, and opened his own shop in Dublin in 1984. The impracticality of a single range shop in the financial climate of the late 1980s and his preoccupation with expansion in the German market brought its closure in 1988. In the same year he became the first designer since Sybil Connolly to be

Left:
PLATE 45 Linen dress and printed silk scarf by John Rocha, 1993. The scarf with its dominant design is an example of the fabric printing which became an important feature of John Rocha's work in the 1990s. Collection Ulster Museum (Photo: Michael Taylor) Model: Shannon, Style Academy

PLATE 46 Jacket by Michael Mortell, part of a strong stylist's outfit for an Elle *fashion feature, 1986. Courtesy ELLE (UK) (Photo: Martin Brading)*

picked for inclusion in the American *Vogue* pattern book for his 'tailoring which is excellent and his good sense of line and structure'.

For the last few years of the eighties he kept a low profile, not staging expensive fashion shows and refusing a Satzenbrau fashion Oscar. He continued to produce excellent collections. In 1990 he decided to concentrate on producing rainwear, mainly for economic reasons, which he has done successfully ever since. He also produces the Michael Mortell Country range, using mostly Irish fabrics. In a precarious profession Michael Mortell is still successfully in business, but had he been lucky enough to have strong financial backing at the right time he could very well now be one of the top international names.

Paul Costelloe's early career which began in the late 1970s has already been mentioned, together with his successful use of Irish fabrics, especially in the early 1980s when he first made his international name. He won the prestigious international *Fil d'Or* award three times,[5] a tribute to his designs in linen. Essentially a day-wear designer, his look can vary from ultra-smart town suits, 'urban chic' as he calls it, to the 'rural chic' of his diffusion range, Dressage, introduced in 1989. In this collection, and his Dressage Jeans collection, natural fibres and landscape colours dominate. As has been said, his tailoring relates to that of Armani, whom he admires greatly.

Mariad Whisker was born in Belfast, into a 'linen family' – all of her great aunts worked in the Blackstaff Linen Mill. She trained in Manchester and sold her own label first in Dublin's Galleria on St Stephen's Green and then opened her own shop in Dawson Street. Sadly, it did not survive but she maintained prestigious outlets in Dublin. For much of the eighties linen was the fabric with which she was most closely associated and she, too won an international award, the *Fil d'Argent* in 1989. Her clothes were unstructured, loose, and usually long. Perfect proportion and precisely the right weight of fabric for the design made her clothes flattering to wear. They had a puritan feel to them in the early eighties as she often used black and white together. Then toning, subtle colours were used as she began to work with viscose. By 1990 she had three labels: her main collection, 'Firenze' by Mariad Whisker, and a diffusion range Dial M. A trip to India was a great new creative stimulus, and in the early nineties much of her range had the stark whiteness one associates with the dress of that country. Mariad won many Irish fashion awards and was featured in UK journals; she seemed poised to move into an expanding market when, faced with the need to move to Los Angeles with her family, she chose to give up a career that was very successful on one level but grindingly hard and financially unrewarding on another. Her creativity has found another outlet in her increasingly successful writing, but everyone connected with the fashion business in Ireland feels very sorry that her individual and strong design talent and flair has not had the international success which seemed so close.

Liz Quin and Carolyn Donnelly are both graduates of the Grafton Academy. Carolyn who was also a fashion writer with the *Irish Press* for seven years started her studio/shop 'Ritzy' in 1978. She was joined by Liz in 1979 and Ritzy Design Studios was formed. Despite critical success, financial difficulties caused them to close for a short time in the late 1980s. Luckily they were commissioned by A-Wear to produce two collections a year in 1989 and they have flourished ever since, concentrating on design while A-Wear deals with production and

PLATE 47 Suit by Mariad Whisker, 1990, which shows her accomplished sense of proportion and strong plain style.
(Photo: Tony Higgins)

marketing. A great advantage to the buying public is that they can sell clothes for less than when they were independent and consequently their collections have a very reasonable, almost chain-store, price range.

Quin & Donnelly's clothes are commercial in the best sense of the word. They are not 'investment' garments, but still work well from

PLATE 48 Short viscose dress by Mariad Whisker, autumn/winter 1992. (Photo: Andrew Hetherington)

season to season, and can be added to each new collection. The tailoring is good, and there is often an unexpected element in the proportion, design or fabric. The unusual use of fabric in particular is a key feature which gives a lift to the simple, easy shapes. The fabrics used include French wools and bouclés, Indian cottons, Irish linens, a variety of Italian fabric mixes, sheepskin and knitwear.

The Quin & Donnelly label now sells to the UK, Europe (where France is the biggest market), Japan and the US. As a general comment, Liz Quin mentions that in recent years there is a marked change in the degree of respect given to Irish fashion by international buyers who take it much more seriously than they did formerly.

Louise Kennedy began her company in 1986. Her style is evolutionary, simple and eminently wearable. Its proportions, colour and fabric combinations, and pleasing small details give it interest and life. The fabrics are typically light mixtures of wool and manmade fibres, English or Italian. A good example of her style is the trouser suit in the collection of the Ulster Museum, bought in 1994,

PLATE 49 Mariad Whisker (standing) and a model both wearing her white outfits, 1995, inspired by a recent trip to India. (Photo: John Swannell)

the year of her successful expansion into English markets. This combines a subtle, interesting combination of patterns, with masculine tailoring softened by a big handpainted scarf. Louise's company has a sound business footing, and her factory production is reliable and of good quality. She has a good home market and has had London outlets from the late 1980s. She has shown with the British Design Group since 1992. She was, therefore, establishing herself in England when she became one of Simpson's key designers in the store's reorganization in 1994. President Mary Robinson wore a Louise Kennedy jacket for her inauguration in 1990.

PLATE 50 Outfit by Quin & Donnelly, 1987, which shows the typically contrasting patterns and materials of their separates. (Photo: Conor Horgan) IMAGE Magazine September 1987

Designers of Clothes – Abroad

Many very talented Irish fashion designers have made their careers abroad. They are successful and significant enough to be considered as a separate section in this study. They now work predominantly in the US and Europe, as well in England, the home of most 1950s expatriate designers. Two of the most long-term successful, Lorcan Mullany and Peter O'Brien, work in London and Paris respectively. These two capitals are the focus for much Irish talent, and so many Irish designers work in Milan that they can be seen as a distinct group. Designers

PLATE 51 Suit by Louise Kennedy, 1994, illustrating the subtlety of pattern and shape details which are typical of her work. Collection Ulster Museum Model: Shannon, Style Academy

whose full-time base is outside Ireland tend to design in a way which is of necessity much less directly referential to their country of origin, though some frequently employ Irish fabrics. Working for an established company also requires the firm's image to be a design consideration. These expatriate designers are less well-known than they deserve to be because many work at a high level in the design teams of international designer companies in a state of relative anonymity.

Lorcan Mullany trained at the Grafton Academy, then moved to London, where he worked with Bill Gibb, Hardy Amies and Ronald Joyce. He produced a collection under his own label, then in 1987 joined the long-established Bellville Sassoon company as designer for the ready-to-wear collections. These are produced under the label Bellville Sassoon-Lorcan Mullany. Elegant or romantic evening wear is the most noteworthy aspect of these collections. The company has a wide clientele including royalty, the aristocracy, socialites and show

PLATE 52 Lorcan Mullany's evening dresses are often darkly romantic, as is this example of 1993. The highlighted detail is a typical feature. Collection Ulster Museum (Photo: Michael Taylor) Model: Claire, Marco Rosala

business personalities. Lorcan Mullany often uses dark colours highlighted by light details. Typical examples are the elegant dress worn by the Princess of Wales and the romantic dress owned by the Ulster Museum, seen in colour plate 11 and plates 52 and 53.

Peter O'Brien's design career began with window dressing at Bests, then Arnotts, in Dublin. He was encouraged to go to London, and was accepted by the prestigious St Martin's School of Art. He graduated

PLATE 53 Sketch by Lorcan Mullany of a short evening dress which was made for the Princess of Wales in winter 1990.
PLATE 54 Sketch by Peter O'Brien of a 1995 evening outfit which shows the sharp detailing, lavish use of fabric and sense of easy style associated with his designs.

with a first-class degree and trained in New York for a year, before going to Paris to look for work. He worked in Dior's and Givenchy's workshops and then went on to design for Chloé after the departure of Karl Lagerfeld. This was a difficult challenge because, as he said, he was damned if his work was like Lagerfeld's and damned if it wasn't! In 1990 he became the designer for the firm of Rochas, which was relaunching its fashion house after a forty-year absence during which it had concentrated on its perfume business. Peter O'Brien produces 'ready-to-wear luxe'. His clothes are of beautiful subtly coloured and subtly cut fabrics, in what the French see as 'Irish' colours. The trimming, intricacy of cut and lavish use of unusual or expensive fabrics makes the clothes unsuitable for mass production, but they are not as formal or ostentatious as those of the grand couture houses. He uses Irish tweeds, such as Tim Roberts' and also reinterprets some of the traditional cloths of his homeland in a very individualistic way. His Aran bustiers and sheath dresses are a far cry from their island roots.

A Northerner, Murray Scallon from Irvinestown in Co. Fermanagh, is another successful Irish designer who, by way of Dublin's National

College of Art and Design (NCAD) and Brussels, now works in Milan. He has, for the last six years, been part of the design team of Erreuno. He still enjoys working for the company, where he is involved in the complete design process, but he has now also realized his ambition to produce a collection under his own label. In June 1994 and November 1995 his collections of simple, lean shapes in a variety of velvets, satins and cottons won praise, particularly for their vibrant colours. Especially in Milan, which Murray and other compatriot designers see as a sartorially conservative city, his clothes have an unexpected exuberance. At present they are only available in Italy, but he hopes that as his own label work expands he can export from his adopted city.

Jim Coughlan from Cork was another Irish/Milanese designer until 1995, when he moved to Paris to work in the Christian Lacroix studio. He now looks after ready-to-wear day wear in a small design team, which suits him well. Jim Coughlan's romantic and luxurious tastes and styles conform easily both to Lacroix's designs and to those of Vivienne Westwood, for whom he previously worked, and whom he found uniquely inspirational. In his college show, Jim reworked the type of dress seen in Jim Sheridan's 1990 film *The Field*, set in mid-twentieth century Ireland, into a high-fashion statement, in the same way that Vivienne Westwood has done with English establishment country dress. He was helped by established firms like 'Cleo' and was able to source original fabrics and yarns. It is no wonder that he feels at home in a house which enjoys using colourful, unusual and rich fabrics. Christian Lacroix himself often uses Irish fabrics, and like so many of the French has a partiality for Ireland and the Irish.

'Ireland represents for me a country of wonders and I feel strangely close to it. I believe this is due to Ireland's very warm and authentic tradition consisting of fine workmanship, popular arts and an informal elegance which is stronger than any fashion. It's my own exoticism!'

CHRISTIAN LACROIX

When he was interviewed as an NCAD student entrant at the Satzenbrau fashion awards in 1987 James Waldron, from Ballyhaunis, Co. Mayo, said, 'I quite like Giorgio Armani[6]'. He is now living in Milan as a senior design assistant to that same man. Even as a student, working in the United States to earn college fees, he was offered orders by Bloomingdales, which was no mean achievement for a neophyte designer. On graduating he went straight to Italy where he worked for some time with Luciano Soprani before joining Armani.

Yet another Irish/Milanese designer is John Connor, who comes from Belfast. He trained at the College of Art and Design there before going to St Martin's School of Art in London. His career since then has been mostly based in Italy. The firms with which he has been most closely connected are Erreuno, and since 1995, Krizia. He is now responsible for the fabric research and realization of five of the lines of this influential fashion company.

Quite a number of Irish designers in Milan have moved to and fro

PLATE 55 Sketch by John Connor of two of his designs for the Italian firm 'Erreuno', autumn/winter 1994.

between fashion-based and other types of design. Nuala Goodman at one time designed for Fiorucci but she has also worked in non-fashion design. Marie Darmody, who worked with Moschino, now has her own design company.

Other Irish 'ghost' designers, who work at a high level for large international companies include Anne Kennedy from Newcastlewest

PLATE 56 Bodice by the American designer Bill Blass, 1992. The embroidery design is by Helen Fitzpatrick who works from near Lurgan, Co. Armagh, for the New York embroidery firm 'Finesse'. New technology now makes such long distance employment possible.

in Co. Limerick, product manager for Lee Cooper's headquarters in Paris; Albert Wong, trained in Belfast and designing for Iceberg; Karen Brennan at Romeo Gigli, then at Jil Sander; Kevin Minogue of Armani; Barry McCuskey of Calvin Klein menswear; Jarlath Mellett of Fenn Wright and Manson. Some designers manage, through modern computer technology, to work in an international context from Ireland. Helen Fitzpatrick used to live in New York working for the famous embroidery firm Finesse. She now lives near Lurgan in Co. Armagh yet still works for the same company. Her designs feature in the work of houses such as Bill Blass, Oscar de la Renta, and Balmain (for whom de la Renta now designs).

Knitwear Designers

The Irish knitwear industry of the 1980s and '90s has built on and greatly expanded the success of the '70s. It is an industry particularly suited to Ireland and especially easy to sell abroad. This happy combination is a result of an adaptable knitwear tradition, appropriate and well-organized production methods, abundant design talent which has adapted to the requirements of a world market, and very good management and marketing.

Knitting is an unusual branch of the fashion business in that it has adapted most successfully to computerized state-of-the-art high technology production methods, yet still requires only two needles and a ball of wool for equally successful home manufacture. Many of Ireland's knitwear designers come from a rural background. They began knitting for a variety of reasons: 'to produce a gift of love' (Lainey Keogh), 'for a bet' (Cyril Cullen), or 'as a childhood pastime' (Edel McBride). Only a few had knitting in the blood, like the Cullen family of West End Knitwear.[7]

The dominant international name in Irish knitwear is Lainey Keogh, followed closely by Edel McBride, Inis Meáin and a veritable host of other producers who began their businesses in the late seventies, eighties or early nineties. These include Glynis Robins, Lyn-Mar, Deirdre Fitzgerald, Joan Millar, Gertrude Sampson, Cyril Cullen and Eily Doolan among many others. Older-established firms such as Micheline Stacpoole still thrive.

Lainey Keogh's early training was in microbiology. She began knitting for friends on commission and her professional career began in 1984 when Michael Mortell asked her to work for his collection.

PLATE 57 An early knitwear design, of 1987, by Lainey Keogh, when her work was strongly coloured and of bulkier yarn than that which she has generally been using in the 1990s. (Photo: Conor Horgan) IMAGE Magazine September 1987

PLATE 58 Child's knitwear by Edel McBride, showing the fur-like fringing which was a strong feature of her work in 1993. (Photo: Chris Neely)

She had a very successful Irish business for the rest of the eighties, using mostly chunky, warm yarns. In the nineties she expanded her market to London. Harvey Nichols, Brown's and, most prestigiously, Joseph, bought her collection. She also sells to the US and to Europe. At present she employs over 300 knitters, but she resists further increased production and mechanization, in order to keep the standards of her work at their present level. Her strength, as is the case with many successful designers, is her continuing design development. Her early work and some more recent pieces reveal the traditional roots of her craft, but an awareness of the changing proportions of fashion and a never-ending investigation into new yarns, yarn finishes and stitches has kept her work continually featured in the international press. American and British *Vogue* regularly illustrate her work. Her sharply coloured velvet knit crop tops, for example, conformed perfectly to the sharp shapes of summer 1994. Her floating deconstructed gossamer knits of the early nineties also form a contrast to the traditional view of Irish knitting.

PLATE 59 Inis Meáin knitwear from the middle Aran Island has great international appeal and is exported very effectively. It retains a strong rural Irish identity, which is evident in an image such as this, of 1994, and in its trademark, an upturned currach (tarred hide boat traditionally used in Galway Bay). (Photo: Mike Bunn)

She has won many awards, the most prestigious being Christian Lacroix's award of the *Prix de Couer* in Monte Carlo in 1989.

Edel McBride's business is based in the old Convoy Woollen Mill in Donegal. She is a graduate of Limerick Regional Technical College, and after some years' experience in the trade she set up her own business in 1987. It has thrived and expanded quickly with a healthy and growing home and export market. While her designs are a conscious blend of Irish/Celtic and Japanese inspiration, which gives a basic proportion and texture, they are contemporary enough to have been used by the British designer Helen Storey for her collections. The use of new international yarns and state-of-the-art Japanese knitting technology means constant new developments for Edel and her large force of outworkers. The use of lycra in her knitwear and an expansion into clothing are interesting new steps. The clothing is simple in shape, but is outstanding for the perfect use of different and unusual fabrics.

Tarlach de Blacam went to live in Inis Meáin (the second largest of the Aran Islands) in 1974 with his wife Aine who was a native of the

PLATE 60 Catwalk shot from the Northern Ireland Satzenbrau Fashion Showcase of 1994, showing Maggie Jackson's 'Maggi Knits' designs. (Photo: Rory Moore) Models: Style Academy

island. They were involved with setting up a co-op on the island to get basic services like running water and electricity. It also set up a knitwear operation which Tarlach de Blacam took over as a separate industry in 1977. He turned the home production of heavy traditional hand-knitted sweaters into an operation which uses the latest computer-aided knitting machinery to produce high-fashion garments. These sell in quantity to the target markets of Japan and Europe. Yohji Yamamoto,[8] for example, sells Inis Meáin knitwear in his boutique. Inis Meáin's well-deserved international success has

PLATE 61 Child's outfit by Eily Doolan, 1988. Eily Doolan was best known at the start of her career for her wedding dress designs but now mostly produces machine and handknits in a luxurious variety of fibres including angora, silk chenille and alpaca. Black and ivory are typical colours.
(Photo: Colm Henry)

PLATE 62 Glynis Robins designs both cloth and knitted garments. This is a simple, effective design worn with a 'Ramsay of Dublin' blouse. The image created is gentle, romantic, nostalgic and historic, all attributes which help market Irish fashion abroad. An Bord Tráchtála/The Irish Trade Board

been achieved by its attention to marketing and selling, the employment of a good consultant designer in Geraldine Clarke, the use of finer yarns such as alpaca from Peru instead of rougher Yorkshire or Irish wool, and the brave adoption of very expensive advanced technology. The company still creates employment on the island, but now for finishers rather than for knitters. As Edel McBride remarked, 'full use of technology can sometimes sustain the employment which it seemed, initially, to threaten.'

In a nice twist of history, Inis Meáin has just produced a new design which derives from the original 1930s Arans; it is much finer than the better-known heavier and chunkier versions of the 1950s and '60s. Tarlach de Blacam with his £1m turnover and expanding business has stemmed the flow of emigration on his island, a fine reward for a successful, if reluctant, capitalist.

Maggie Jackson has always, except for a short career break, worked in Northern Ireland where she is the most successful designer of knitwear. Her company Maggi Knits, founded in 1977, was Northern Ireland's first fashion design company. At that time, there was not even a model agency in Northern Ireland. She is living proof that design and business skills can co-exist. Her designs use a variety of yarns but are most associated with Herdman's linen thread. They are strikingly textural, with reference to traditional Aran stitches, but are contemporary in style. During the eighties Maggie built up her own company (in 1989 she won the Northern Ireland Young Business and Professional Woman of the Year title and was runner-up in the UK), and also worked hard for fashion in Northern Ireland. She was Chairman of the Northern Ireland Fashion Designers' Association and was an instigator in setting up the Fashion Business Centre.

In 1992, after illness had forced a career break, Maggie set up the company again. She completed an international marketing and management course in Boston, and a placement in Nieman Marcus, and altered the focus of the firm. She changed what had been basically a cottage industry by concentrating on greater production, and building up the export market. She now has fifty outworkers, her business thrives again and she exports to the UK, America, Japan, Germany and Egypt.

I have detailed the careers of only four of Ireland's most successful knitwear designers, from four different parts of Ireland. Many more deserve mention, and have entries in the directory at the back of the book. Some of their work, such as that of Joan Millar, Eily Doolan and Glynis Robins, can be seen in the plates.

By the end of the 1980s Ireland's top fashion designers had made their mark on the international fashion world, and many more had built up strong national reputations, which in most cases would expand in the 1990s.

5 THE FASHION SYSTEM

It is a truism that nothing exists in a vacuum. The fashion industry in Ireland is affected by a myriad of social, economic, historic, legislative and accidental circumstances – some are helpful, some not, most simply move the business in one direction or other. Designer fashion is an integral part of a greater totality, the clothing trade of Ireland. One can imagine this trade as a pyramid composed of three layers.

The bottom and widest layer is the CMT factory trade – the 'cut make and trim' industry which employs 15,000 in Northern Ireland and 10,000 in the Republic of Ireland and accounts for 65 per cent of all clothing exports. These are mostly Ireland's hidden exports, since they are made for well-known brands in the UK. Large companies such as Paul Sharma of Nena Models in Donegal, for example, make for the likes of Principles and Richard Shops as well as Irish chain stores such as Dunnes, and Desmonds of Derry makes for Marks and Spencer. There are very many smaller operations in the north and south.

The middle layer of the pyramid consists of the manufacturing firms who have their own brand names. They produce high quality goods, for both home and export markets, in large quantity. Their product images, created by in-house design teams are perhaps not very distinctive, but this suits the level of international market to which they aspire. Sometimes these firms make their own designs (and may also manufacture for other designers), and sometimes they use other Irish, UK or even Far Eastern CMT production. The finalists in the Fashion Industry Achievement Award section of the Late Late Show Fashion Awards of 1995 – Loretta Bloom, Michael H, Michel Ambers, Libra and Santorini – are examples of such companies. At the very top level of this layer there is little to distinguish the market or the quality of the product from that of the designer label company. Apart from the couturiers' output all clothing is ready-to-wear and many old established firms such as Henry White maintain very high standards of tailoring and finishing. Some of these firms, too, have permanent designers such as Helen McAlinden and Linda Byrne of Ramsay of Dublin whose personal handwriting creates the firm's look. A contemporary or traditional decision to promote the

PLATE 63 Outfit by Henry White, 1996, showing the tailoring and design skills of this long-established family firm.
(Photo: Mike Bunn)

brand name rather than the designer's name, however, means that these firms are not personality-led. Helen McAlinden, in fact, feels that the idea of the 'designer label' was overdone in the 1980s, and that brand names such as Gucci or Prada are very successful examples of the ability of brand names to create their own cachet just as effectively.

At the tip of the pyramid are the designer label firms who may work on a large scale with an entrenched international profile, or on a smaller scale with a merely national renown and an incipient export market. Their most important characteristic is that they are the image makers, and that they both fulfil and extend international expectations of Irish fashions. They are, to a greater or lesser extent, at the cutting edge of international fashion, and it is this context within which they work. The top design companies and operations may be as diverse in scale, material and production method as Lainey Keogh, Paul Costelloe and Philip Treacy but they are all alike in having a clear design image and an international reputation.

All three layers of the pyramid are to some extent interdependent – the top layer may depend on the expertise of the lower levels for production, and the lower layers are helped by the image-makers'

PLATE 64 Hacking jacket by Ramsay of Dublin, 1995, one of the most perennially successful designs of the firm. The firm's designers, Helen McAlinden and Linda Byrne, usually include some garments of Irish fabric and spirit among their collections aimed at an international export market. (Photo: Barry McCall)

design successes. All are bound by the same necessities – they must design, make, promote, and sell successfully to keep in business.

DESIGN

Successful design is not just about aesthetic sensibility, original ideas and an understanding of fashion, important though these are. Few designers have the luxury of designing purely for self-expression, without constraint by the economic realities of their trade. They must consider the market they are aiming for, the price of materials and production, and make sure that the purse of one is appropriate to the costs of the other. Maggie Jackson claims with good reason that in a successful fashion business, design skills count for 40 per cent and business skills 60 per cent, and a similar opinion is expressed by most designers. A designer not lucky enough to have a business partner or backer who can take on this 60 per cent must do this for him or herself. Business skills are not conventionally associated with creativity, but the latter cannot survive without the former.

'Fashion is like a four-legged table: you need a good designer, a very good business manager, a good manufacturer and a very good distributor. Without all the legs, table collapses.'

JOHN ROCHA

The Colleges of Art and Design in the Republic of Ireland and Northern Ireland have, over the past few decades, heavily emphasized the realities of business practice to fashion students. Most colleges are fortunate in having very dedicated staff, many of whom have had practical experience in the fashion trade. Patricia Keilthy and Pam McCarthy of Limerick Regional Technical College, Frances McDonagh of NCAD (Dublin's National College of Art and Design), Olive Clegg, recently retired from UU (the University of Ulster) and their staff are some of the teachers who have fought hard and long, and usually in the face of financial constraint, to exploit every opportunity for their students. Every year there are a few outstanding pupils who justify this expense of spirit and commitment.

Ireland also has excellent private fashion design colleges with a fine track record of producing successful designers. The Grafton Academy of Dress Designing founded by Mrs. Pauline Clotworthy, and now run by her daughter Mrs Suzanne Marr, has a remarkable output of graduates which has included Ib Jorgensen, Paul Costelloe, Lorcan Mullany, Clodagh and Louise Kennedy. The Barbara Bourke Academy and others also have notable past pupils. New fashion courses at regional colleges such as Mallow's also have had early successes. It is debatable, however, whether the plethora of new courses at regional technical colleges are realistically attuned to considerations of the practical career prospects of

PLATE 65 'Behind the scenes' photograph taken at a Paul Costelloe fashion show, 1994. (Photo: Nick Tucker)

their many students. Colleges now include courses in business skills, but a general complaint is that they still, taken as a whole, tend to give insufficient emphasis to the requirements of industry.

Left:
PLATE 66 A beautifully cut and finished day suit by Ib Jorgensen, 1992.
(Photo: Tony Higgins)

PRODUCTION

The efficient and economic production of a design is often problematic. An in-house workroom, such as a couturier might have, probably gives rise to least difficulties. Staff in such situations are typically highly trained, work to a very high standard, and at a very high speed. Traditionally, they were paid poorly, but their skills are now better rewarded. Regrettably there is less demand than in the past for their specialist abilities. With rare exceptions, such as the newcomer Jen Kelly, most couturiers are facing retirement.

The knitwear designer, too, typically has a well-organized production network, mostly based on a cottage industry system which is becoming more and more mechanized. The traditional out-knitters appear to have adapted well to domestic mechanization. Today some firms such as Inis Meáin are fully computerized and mechanization produces the knitting, handworkers now only finishing the garments. Edel McBride even foresees a time when Japanese Shima Seiki machines will run 24 hours a day in homes, operated on a shift system by different members

PLATE 67 Section of the factory floor of J.N. Clarke Ltd, c. 1968, showing hand finishing of coats and suits. Jack Clarke's ready-to-wear coats and suits were produced to the high standard that would now be associated with made-to-measure clothes.
(Photo: Walter Pfeiffer)

of the family, something that happens to some extent in Italy already.

Most designer-label clothing firms use Irish CMT firms to produce their ranges. Quality is reasonably high, although there is a limited number who are of top rank. Quality control is sometimes a problem, as is the lack of investment capital for new machinery. Finding good quality CMT firms, especially for a designer who produces a small range needing only a few months' work, can be extremely difficult.

Many observers foresee that the increasing trend for production to shift to cheaper overseas workforces is inevitable. However the Irish CMT industry does have advantages which can help it to survive. It is a reliable industry which can produce goods on time at a reasonable price, in small quantities, without lengthy advance notice and can easily repeat orders. In addition, if a UK client, for example, has a pressing problem, they are probably only an hour away by air from the production line. Also, for UK, Irish or, increasingly, European clients, there is no language barrier. The labour costs of Far Eastern clothing production are certainly a fraction of those of Ireland but are best exploited by big organizations, since Eastern companies typically deal most advantageously with very large orders for which a six-month setting-up period may be needed. Again, if problems arise, they are exacerbated by language difficulties and the 18-hour journey by air.

Areas of cheap labour in or near the EU such as Portugal and Turkey are of much more potential danger to the Irish industry. Even in the UK, wages are less than in Ireland.

PROMOTION

Promotion for the industry has also, in the opinion of many, suffered from a lack of quality control. Government bodies on the whole are not in a position to consider artistry, creativity and originality as qualities worthy of promotion above and beyond the potential of quantity export. This is either seen as right and proper in the light of economic reality, or as hopelessly conservative since it denies inducement to trailblazing efforts which will drag the whole industry forward in its wake. Sometimes designers feel that help other than that on offer would be more effective. For example, several designers I have spoken to have considered that an interest-free set-up loan would be of more use than a grant of a few thousand pounds towards a trade show or fashion show. Most, however, take a pragmatic viewpoint that any help is worth having, but that they basically must sink or swim on their own. Heavy VAT rates on clothing, raised in 1993 to 21 per cent in the Republic of Ireland, and, even more problematic, its heavy taxation on the employment of permanent staff are also seen as burdens which the trade could do without. The couturiers in particular were incensed by the VAT, which was seen as a significant deterrent to purchase at couture price levels (even though they are relatively low in Ireland). Ib Jorgensen saw it as the final straw in persuading him to retire from fashion and devote himself to his Fine Art business, and Thomas Wolfangel too, feels strongly that it is detrimental to his craft.

Every government body, north and south is, of course, subject to the irreconcilable difficulties of infinite demands on finite resources. The continuing reliability or otherwise of funding sources is usually the determining factor in the success or failure of most government schemes.

In Northern Ireland, for example, the IDB (Industrial Development Board) helps and promotes large businesses, and LEDU (Local Enterprise Development Unit) smaller companies. The province also offers specific help to clothing designers and manufacturers, which grew out of the Northern Ireland Fashion Designers Association. This association was formed in the early 1980s by a group of fashion designers practising as individual companies, initiated by Maggie Jackson (Maggi Knits), Carole Cairns and Colleen Tilson (Pink Inc), Margaret Lismore, Geraldine Connon, Margaret Annett and Kathryn Morrison. They aimed to create a pressure group to gain recognition and financial support for the members' businesses, and worked to develop entrepreneurship and common resources, in particular a manfacturing base. With support from LEDU and the International Fund for Ireland they established themselves in Belfast premises under the name of the Fashion Design Centre.

A chief executive and a small staff were employed to provide business facilities, a research and marketing service, computerized pattern cutting and grading and start-up studio/workshop spaces. The centre also provided training programmes in marketing skills and trend forecasting for small clothing companies. FINS[1], the national/international on-line designer database was installed in the centre for use by Northern Ireland manufacturers in 1994.

In 1994, the International Fund for Ireland's decision not to continue support for ongoing projects created a shortfall in funding which LEDU was unable to make good. Unfortunately, the centre had not been fully operational long enough to generate sufficient income to be independent, so it closed. However, several of the original members of the Fashion Designers' Association, together with others, continue to offer design, prototype and small manufacturing services from the former centre's premises in McAvoy House in Ormeau Avenue.

The Clothing Development Centre (CDC) was set up to provide a more extensive manufacturing facility, the need having been highlighted by the growth of small, designer-led businesses in the province. This was set up in West Belfast with funding made available under the Making Belfast Work scheme.

In the Republic of Ireland 'Forbairt' is the government body which now aids indigenous businesses with start-up, management and technological help and advice. IDA helps with bringing in foreign businesses and investment. Certain bodies help specific areas such as Shannon Development for the Shannon region, Udaras na Gaeltachta for the Irish-speaking Gaeltacht areas, etc. There is no specific government body to help the fashion industry, but An Bord Tráchtála, the Irish Trade Board (the descendant of the Dollar Board, Coras Tráchtála)[2] does have specific sections which provide many of the facilities offered by a combination of the CBC and LEDU in the North. Practical help is given to clothing manufacturing companies, such as cutting and layout advice, fashion forecasting and supplying product specialists who can help get the product right for markets, especially export markets. The knitwear industry in particular benefited from these services. Significant help is also available in limited circumstances through the TMC Scheme (Targeted Marketing Consultancy).

Trade organizations, which are mostly support, pressure and marketing groups also help the fashion industry. The Irish Fashion Group, for example, was set up in the mid-1970s as a cooperative selling group which also disseminates information on credit control, fashion forecasting, etc. Most of the members of this group are 'not in the ethnic end of the business', as the chairman, Brian Beggan of Libra, so succinctly puts it. The Irish Knitwear Exporters Guild started in 1985 with a membership of seven companies. Now there are twenty-three, responsible for about £35 million worth of Irish knitwear export sales out of an Irish total of around £62 million.

Promotions for Irish fashion include the Look to our Own scheme and various retail-based promotions in Ireland and elsewhere. A difficulty in any promotion tends to be in defining the level of the product which is promoted. Exclusivity is self-defeating, but to include every firm diffuses the message, introducing the lowest common denominator factor, and reduces the overall perceived quality to the detriment of the creative originals. 'Showcase', a huge exhibition of craft and fashion for home and export buyers, is held every January in the Royal Dublin Society exhibition area in Dublin. It is organized by the Crafts Council of Ireland. The last Showcase generated enormous export business. In the north of Ireland, Craftworks provides a retail outlet, exhibition space and advice for designers whose work spans the fashion/craft divide.

SELLING

No industry can survive unless it can sell its goods effectively. Ireland suffers from local, national and global problems as far as selling fashion is concerned, but it also enjoys some advantages.

Ireland, with its relatively small population cannot provide a big enough market to sustain its fashion industry alone, hence the necessary emphasis on export promotion. Such a market as there is is heavily concentrated in Dublin. The size of the country is such that Dublin can serve as a place for occasional shopping for almost the whole country. Cork, Limerick, Belfast and Galway and Sligo are also important regional shopping centres. They all, like Dublin, have the full range of UK High Street chain stores (a situation which demonstrates the domination of the large British and European retail giants) which reduces the home market for Irish goods. They do not have quite the same size of market, however, for designer-led fashion as Dublin, but even Dublin has never, up to the present, been able to sustain a single-designer shop.

One advantage the home market does have is the added buying power of the ever-expanding tourist trade. This probably helps the high fashion knitwear market most.

Given this small market, it has to be said that there is quite a wide variety of retail opportunities for fashion designers in Ireland. At the top end of the market there are the private clients. These may be the traditional wealthy socialite customers of the couturiers, or the media and show business customers of, for example, Jen Kelly or Marc O'Neill.

Young designers have potential outlets such as the Design Centre in Powerscourt Townhouse Centre in Dublin which provides units for twenty designers. It sells work by established designers and also by new young designers just out of art college, in the Innovative Designer Forum section. Most contemporary Irish designers have passed through the Design Centre at one stage of their career.

Work of established Irish designers is also sold in specialist fashion shops such as Havana of Donnybrook, run by Nicky Creeden, ex-manager of the Design Centre, Diffusion of Clontarf and Khan of Blackrock. Shops selling club wear and young designers work thrive in most Irish cities. 'Se Si' in Dublin is a good example. Those department stores which remain continue to be supporters of Irish fashion, as shown by the spectacular 1996 show of Irish Fashion Design at the Point Theatre organized by Brown Thomas. Some department stores have begun concession selling, where the designers supply stock and staff for their own area.

Two recent developments in particular give great support to

selected designers. The A-Wear chain of shops (subsumed into the Brown Thomas Group), of which Mrs Deirdre Kelly was the managing director,[3] gives selected designers their own label and organizes production, selling and marketing for them. John Rocha (who has recently left the A-Wear stable) and Quin & Donnelly are the best-known designers whose careers have been greatly helped by A-Wear. Marc O'Neill joined the group in 1995, so he too now has the luxury of being able to concentrate on design work.

A somewhat similar set-up exists with the company Sasha, whose merchandise is all designed by Irish designers, and is made in Ireland. It does not promote the designers' names in the same way, however, although Aine McDonnell has her 'Aine at Sasha' label.

Blarney Woollen Mills is a family-run company based in County Cork, which has expanded to eight country-wide outlets. It bought over the Kilkenny Design Shop (now The Kilkenny Shop) in Dublin in 1989 where it continues to sell top Irish design products. Within this store it sells its own range of fashion under the label Kilkenny Art of Dressing designed by Oonagh Moriarty, but also sells top-of-the-range clothes by Irish designers and manufacturers such as Ramsay of Dublin, Henry White, Lyn-Mar, Louise Kennedy and new designer ranges such as Allicano. The other stores sell a more limited range of Irish manufactured clothing, and they all a sell large quantity of their own label and other designers' knitwear, such as that of Edel McBride, Glynis Robin, and Lainey Keogh. Much of the tweed used is Irish, and the company works with weavers to achieve the right fabrics.

A few companies manage successfully to combine all activities from fabric production to garment making to promotion. The best known of these is Avoca Handweavers, now run by the Pratt family who acquired the long-established but run-down mill in 1974 from the solicitor who bought it from the elderly Misses Wynn. Car rugs, which had become expendable in modern cars, had been the firm's main product, made from distinctively woven mohair. The Pratts began to make this fabric up into a small range of garments, adding more designs in a greater variety of weaves and weights over the years. Though the firm no longer dyes, it still weaves its own cloth (mostly by power loom but retaining some hand weaving). A factory unit on its premises at Kilmacanogue, near Bray, Co. Wicklow, makes up the cloth beside its large attractive tourist centre shop which sells Avoca and other Irish products. A knitting unit supplies this shop and the five others in Ireland, all attractively situated in tourist areas. A healthy export trade backs up the home market.

The production of this clothing range which makes use of all local advantages from on-the-spot fabrics to Ireland's attraction to tourists seems an ideal set-up and one could visualize other similar operations. It depends for its success, however, on a close-knit, mostly family team, a manageable company size, and on great marketing skills which have a large but precise target market. This combination is not easily found.

A designer *can* survive independently in Ireland outside Dublin selling to the home market with a small workforce and production range. Most, however, have to seek a niche market to do this. Examples from the north of Ireland are Winnie Magee with rainwear, Cathy Shannon with hats, Endymion (Patricia Gavin) with printed fabrics and Wendy Smyth with Smyth and Gibson linen shirts. It is significant, though, that of all Northern Ireland's fashion designers, including Jen Kelly, Miriam Mone, Mariad Whisker and Murray Scallon, only Michelle O'Doherty and Maggie Jackson have built strong businesses on their home ground. The rest have gone to Dublin or abroad. A small-scale garment designer in a non-cosmopolitan centre has to beware of the risk of becoming trapped in a situation whereby loyal customers begin to dictate the type of the design to the ultimate boredom and disillusionment of the designer.

On the whole, however, any size of operation, whether it is directed to mass market or niche market must try to export if it wishes to survive and expand. Even when one takes away the 'hidden exports', clothing made in Ireland under contract to the British chain stores, the UK is still the biggest export market for Irish fashion at every level. The quantity of clothing and footwear exports from Ireland to the UK is second only to that from Hong Kong. It is a long-established market of most of the high quality manufacturing companies. Designer label companies such as Lainey Keogh, Paul Costelloe, Louise Kennedy, John Rocha and others all have prestigious outlets there, mostly in specialist departments of fashion stores, and many more have outlets scattered over the country in high quality specialist designer shops.

The Irish Trade Board concentrates its efforts now on the European market, partly because of EU membership and the lack of customs, tariffs and quotas, and partly because within 600 miles is a potential market of 600 million people. After the UK, Germany, followed by France, are the biggest markets for Irish clothing. Italy too is a good market because of the affection for 'traditional' British styles which encompasses a love of Irish knitwear, tweeds and other fabrics.

Outside Europe, Japan is a market which has been sympathetic to Irish goods since the days of Donald Davies' world success. The inroads made by the Irish Tourist Board have helped open Japanese eyes to Ireland and Irish products. A certain natural affinity exists particularly between Irish knitwear design and Japanese dress design. Dress designers who work in a non-structured way, such as Mary Gregory, sell well in Japan. So too do designers who use traditional Irish tweeds.

The United States is relatively speaking much less important as an export market than it used to be. It takes, for example, only about 10 per cent of all knitwear exports now. Adoption by a big store in the States can still be a pathway to financial success but these stores are themselves feeling the recession and reducing their outlay. Many Americans do, however, remain very loyal private clients to Irish couturiers.

Australia is an important potential market, which used to buy quantities of Irish fashion, but quotas and tariffs now make trade difficult. The same problems exist with South American trade. Markets in the southern hemisphere would be very advantageous because they would double the selling period of seasonal products such as winter woollens and summer linens. The former Soviet Union is a very new market, being explored by Brian Beggan of Libra.

One disadvantage of a trade that is primarily export is that competition for markets becomes increasingly intense. Increasingly, too, global factors which are totally unpredictable determine which commercial ventures succeed and which fail. Third World developments, the natural changes in fashion's emphasis, changing customer lifestyles, international trade conditions and unseasonal weather can easily destroy a perfectly efficient industry. These militating factors can be well exemplified by the recent fortunes of one of the fabric industries which underpins the clothing industries – the linen industry.

European linen production is being threatened, firstly, by the long-term fall in demand both for household linen, as has been mentioned before, and the recent reduction in demand from the fashion business.[4] The second danger is the flooding of the market with cheaply produced Chinese linen which is grown, spun and woven in a country where wages are very low. The industry must produce the easy-care fabric the market demands, so a wide variety of fabric blends must be produced in order to survive. This runs the risk of reducing the 'linenness' of linen, its very selling point. Special finishes and weaves must continually be developed to maintain the appeal of linen, and to distinguish it from the rival cheap oriental product. New customers for this quality fabric must be found, but vital expansion to new markets is hampered by tariffs.[5]

The Irish fashion exporter, faced with contradictions and problems such as this, has one great advantage – the indefinable power of image. Even within the hard-pressed linen business, for example, the 'Irish Linen' label has a cachet and selling ability which is unique. Many designers and firms use Irish fabrics in every range, or Irish references, and the quality and 'feel' of their products is often perceived as Irish. The worldwide appetite for Irish culture is again an indefinable advantage which gives Irish merchandise singular appeal. In the cut-throat world of fashion no one is going to buy Irish produce just for the sake of it, but to have a strong personality in the midst of growing international blandness is a necessary first step to successful marketing. Marketing consultants time and again stress the importance of maintaining an Irish identity.

Successful professional marketing, which takes advantage of this identity, is increasingly the key to a profitable business. Finding the right 'price point' for the product, knowing what ranges are going to be in competition, getting the right retail outlet, and procuring the right publicity are vital. A flash of inspiration, such as the use of a currach as a display prop at a trade show in Japan by Tarlach de Blacam, can make a crucial difference to sales. Packaging too can be very important. Part of the appeal of Smyth and Gibson linen shirts is their enticing old-fashioned cardboard box containers. Several

PLATE 68 Linen shirts by Smyth and Gibson, 1996. Wendy Smyth's beautifully packaged high quality linen shirts are proof of the importance of well-planned marketing. They have sold very well in cosmopolitan quality retail outlets. (Photo: Chris Hill)

designers have mentioned how necessary all this expertise is and how useful professional help can be. Other designers who have acquired these skills themselves, or have found others to supply it, have seen business expand rapidly. The skills are very specific – until recently marketing professionals often did not know about or empathize sufficiently with the vagaries of the clothing industry.

THE MEDIA

Locally produced high fashion and lifestyle magazines are relative newcomers to Ireland. *Image* was the first of its kind, founded in 1976 when its publishers saw a gap in the market for a magazine which covered Irish fashion. *IT*, the old-established *Irish Tatler,* was transformed into a similar magazine in the late eighties and since 1995 has concentrated heavily on fashion coverage. These and other magazines like *U* and *Northern Woman* (although its targeted public is much more localized) are aimed at the *Vogue*, *Marie Claire* or *Elle* market, but show clothes that are available in Ireland. They see the promotion of Irish fashion as part of their remit, but only on merit, not as an obligation.

These magazines have all been a focus for the activities of Irish photographers, hairstylists, stylists, and models, many of whom have moved on to international careers. Models such as Aly Dunne became one of the most successful catwalk models of her generation (although not conforming to the ideal mostly required by Irish clients). Betty Wall has been stylist for many influential fashion shoots over the years. Isabella Stanhope, one of the successful international stylists, comes from Ireland (*see* colour plate 15). The stylist Sonya Lennon is best known for her work with the group Boyzone.

The standard of fashion photography in Ireland has always been high and continues to be so. The photographs for this book have been chosen initially for their content, to illustrate a particular designer's typical work. As far as possible we have also tried to use strong images which are good examples of fashion photography. Photographers such as Tony Higgins, Mike Bunn, Conor Horgan, Ursula Steiger, Chris Hill and Barry McCall who have taken many of these all have their own distinctive signature. Tony Higgins' collection shoots dominated in the 1960s and '70s, and he continues to be in demand. Mike Bunn, who began to work in Ireland in the early eighties, just at the time when the Irish fashion business was enjoying a renaissance and new magazines had been set up, created some of the strongest images of Irish fashion in the eighties and nineties. A host of young photographers have successfully started businesses in the nineties. This is despite the fact that many designers cannot afford the

PLATE 69 Designs from the first collection by John Rocha to be shown in London, 1984. (Photo: Mike Bunn)

collection photography that used to be a financial mainstay of the freelance photographer.

Irish fashion has been served well by its journalists, past and present. All have been well-informed and committed and some have an extraordinary breadth of knowledge about the business. Since 1950 their lifestyles and prose styles have changed, their optimism about Irish fashion has waxed and waned, and fashion itself has undergone many an upheaval, but their enthusiasm stays the same. The Irish fashion journalist has remained as a constant support (and occasional scourge) to the Irish designer. If it is not invidious to try to sum up the opinions of such a diverse group of people, most consider that Irish designers, to survive, must continue to find their own individual niche rather than try to compete with a very broad international market.

The broadcasting media has taken fashion more and more seriously over the last decade or so. Magazine programmes which specifically cover contemporary fashion such as *The Clothes Show* in the UK and RTE's *Head 2 Toe* have been both long-running and successful. *Head 2 Toe* covers Irish and international fashion. Its researcher Mary McLaughlin has pointed out that the show itself has become a fashion archive. Eight years ago when it began, the format, style of presentation and presenters were all as much of another age as the content. It is evidence of the growing sophistication of image-making in Ireland, which has gone hand in hand with the increasing professionalism of the fashion industry.

Since the seventies, financial and critical encouragement has been given to Irish designers through the setting up of national and international awards. The International Wool Secretariat was set up in response to the threat to the wool trade from the manmade fibre industry. As part of its successful promotion of wool it gave international awards to designers who used wool. Michelina Stacpoole and Lainey Keogh were two Irish recipients. For some years, while it had a branch in Ireland, under the energetic marketing control of Eddie Shanahan, it also gave national awards. The *Confédération Européenne*

PLATE 70 'Ecdysis' by Wendi Hoey. This outfit won the prestigious Smirnoff International Fashion Award 1993. (Photo: Kip Carroll)

du Lin et du Chanvre (Masters of Linen – the European linen promotional body) gave a prestigious prize in the eighties, the *Fil d'Or*, at an award ceremony in Monte Carlo. Paul Costelloe and Mariad Whisker were both winners in the 1980s, as has been mentioned, and Kathy Boner won the equivalent *Fil d'Or* student award in 1983.

Since 1985 Satzenbrau awards have been given annually to student designers of partywear. In 1988 Satzenbrau's first annual fashion Oscars were presented in Dublin to best designer, best photographer, best model, and best buyer. This award system lasted until 1992. The Satzenbrau Fashion Designer Awards in the north of Ireland, awarded since 1992 are given to student designers of clothing, commercial designers of clothing and commercial designers of accessories.

The long-standing Smirnoff Young Designer Award started in England in 1984 and has grown in scale every year. Winners of the Irish award have the opportunity of meeting international competition in the Smirnoff International Fashion Awards, set up in 1991. Thirty-six countries participated in 1995, and every year the event expands. In 1993 Wendi Hoey from Drogheda won the overall title with her outfit called 'Ecdysis'. (This included a full-length velvet coat which was dipped in bleach and scorched to achieve a decayed effect. It was worn with a cropped muslin top and a long skirt of the same material, which was painted with shellac. The skirt was supported by a crinoline: *see* plate 70). This was a great achievement, against strong opposition, and an enormous boost for Irish student fashion. Winning awards such as this may not be a guarantee of a job for life, but they are still probably a proof that at some level, the fashion system in Ireland works.

6 INTERNATIONAL LIFT-OFF: THE 1990S

It is difficult to be totally objective about the present. A little distance in time is always useful to enable one to distinguish a flash in the pan from the start of a new and important trend. This is true whether one is considering science, art or commerce, or that fusion of all three, fashion. Irish fashion in the nineties does, however, already seem to have some specific features and one can perhaps predict a little of its future.

In the 1990s Ireland has, on the whole, enjoyed a good press. In 1990 Senator Mary Robinson[1] was inaugurated as President of Ireland for a seven-year term. As one of the most able people to have held this office, she has enhanced the image of her country. Her professionalism extends to the very effective promotion of Irish fashion. She wears only Irish designers' work on all state occasions. This has given Irish fashion an international profile at a high diplomatic level and also constant press coverage at home and abroad where it is constantly favourably compared with Parisian fashion. Determinedly even-handed, she has promoted the work of all Irish designers of note in this way.

Awareness of the cultural traditions of Ireland was unexpectedly raised by the phenomenal success of *Riverdance*.[2] The international appeal of this extraordinary show has helped to make Irish dance traditions as well known and respected as Irish traditional music is already. The Irish couturier Jen Kelly designed the costumes for the show.

Ireland's international cultural standing was increased by the award to Seamus Heaney of the Nobel Prize for Literature in 1995. Indeed, the enormous wave of genuine pleasure and pride within Ireland that greeted the announcement did itself underline the fact that the country remains unusually literate, with a strong cultural identity. Since the peace of autumn 1994, Ireland and the previously neglected Northern Ireland have become 'fashionable'. Media, tourist and business interest in the island as a whole has increased enormously. As I write this, the peace has become precarious, and much of the optimism for the future of Ireland, north and south, depends on its survival.

PLATE 71 Inauguration photograph of President Mary Robinson wearing a Louise Kennedy jacket, 1990. (Photo: Conor Horgan)

In the world of fashion some figures have vanished and new talents have appeared. Infuriated by the government's increase in VAT on clothing to 21 per cent, Ib Jorgensen shut his couture house. This imposition was a hard blow for all designers, and cut into dangerously small profit margins, but it particularly affected labour-intensive businesses with a high unit cost. Mariad Whisker has left Ireland for Los Angeles after twenty years in the trade, and is much missed. In the north of Ireland, 'Pink Inc' – Carole Cairns and Colleen Tilson – a successful duo for ten years who had a design and manufacturing base in Northern Ireland and a retail outlet in London succumbed to the recession in the early nineties.

PLATE 72 Jen Kelly's costumes for Riverdance *(Photo: Chris Hill)*

CLOTHES DESIGNERS

Of the 'new' designers of the nineties described in this chapter, some have begun their careers in this decade, while others are discussed here because their careers, which may have begun much earlier, have only now come to fruition. In a book of this scope, given the present quantity and variety of new fashion businesses, inclusion and omissions must appear arbitrary, particularly to those who do not appear in it. I have concentrated on those who have won top awards, been chosen for prestigious fashion events or have been in business long enough to have earned some degree of national or international reputation. Undoubtedly even by the time of publication important new designers will have come to the fore.

Marc O'Neill is a good example of an emerging young Irish designer for whom the future seems set fair. He has been a Smirnoff Fashion Award finalist, and in 1993 was given a student bursary and named Fashion Graduate of the Year by the Society of Designers in Ireland. In 1995, at the age of twenty-four, he joined A-Wear, which allows him freedom to design, unconstrained by production and marketing problems, and gives him a high profile which he will undoubtedly exploit. Already he has appeared with the best and most established

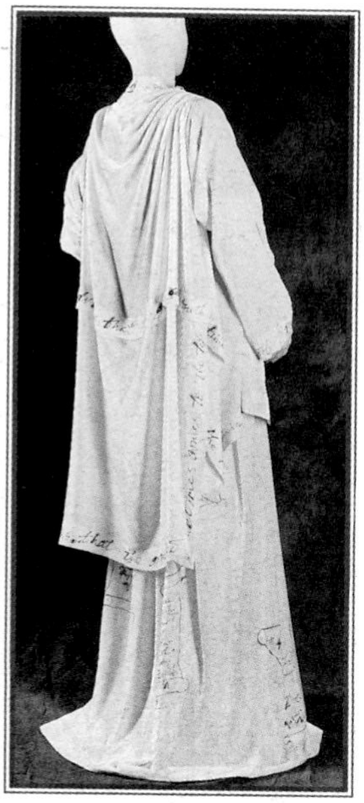

PLATE 73 Velvet outfit by Mary Gregory, 1995. The rich plain fabric, simple but well-proportioned shapes, clever cutting and hand-painted embellishment (a painted quotation from Virginia Woolf, 'It is in our idleness, in our dreams, that the submerged truth sometimes comes to the top') are all hallmarks of Mary Gregory's style. Collection Ulster Museum

PLATE 74 Man's shantung suit by Marc O'Neill, 1996. (Photo: Eamonn McLoughlin)

PLATE 75 Jen Kelly's striking evening outfit of 1992.
(Photo: Barry McCall)

PLATE 76 Linen and crochet outfit by Mary Gregory, 1994.
(Photo: Ronan O'Raw)

PLATE 77 Velvet dress by Michelle O'Doherty, 1995.
(Photo: Jim Crone) Model: Style Academy

PLATE 78 A loose easy knitwear design, 1995, by Deirdre Fitzgerald. (Photo: Barry McCall)

PLATE 79 Brid Nihill is best known for her lavish evening wear, thanks to dresses such as this. (Photo: Barry McCall) IMAGE Magazine October 1995

Irish designers who showed at the Brown Thomas Showcase of Irish Fashion Design at the Point Theatre in February 1996.

This did not come about solely through talent and luck. Marc O'Neill is also professional, organized, and totally aware of the requirements of business and the market. His postgraduate courses in Design Management and Marketing and his wide range of design experience show his commitment to his trade. He has wide knowledge of the fashion business in Ireland generally and sees close collaboration between designers and retailers as the healthiest road for Irish fashion. An important element of his work derives from his contacts and work with other artists such as photographers, graphic artists, dancers and musicians, which result in less formal, often commissioned designs, which help keep his ideas fresh.

Jen Kelly, too, appeared in the Point show and also has clients and interests in the world of the theatre and show business. He was brought up in Derry and had business, marketing and design training and design experience before going to NCAD to study fashion. After a few years of designing and teaching he set up a successful small-scale couture business in 1989 in Molesworth Street in Dublin. He has a staff of two stitchers, plus the backup of a master tailor and milliner when necessary, and has built up a clientele which appreciates the beautiful finish of his clothes. His work is sophisticated and his fabrics are typically rich and fine, mostly from Milan. He also uses Donegal and other Irish tweeds, usually in a sharply tailored cut. Jen's *Riverdance* costumes are his most conspicuously visible designs to date, but he has a host of show-business and other private clients.

The greatest concentration of contemporary Irish fashion designers' work is probably found at The Design Centre in Powerscourt Townhouse Centre in Dublin. Some twenty designers sell there but of those not already mentioned elsewhere I can only name a few, award-winning designers.

Mary Gregory was one of the great successes of the Point show, and since then has found her profile to be significantly raised. She trained in a design company before becoming one of the founder members of The Design Centre in 1984. Her career began slowly and steadily and it is only in the nineties that she has rightly come to be seen as one of the most interesting of contemporary designers. She uses a small palette of exquisite and subtle unpatterned colours in beautiful and rich fabrics. From these she produces superbly tailored and finished garments whose proportion is sometimes unexpected and always perfect. Her recent collections including unstructured garments make her seem a natural successor to Mariad Whisker. The use of lovely fabrics – linens, velvets, silks, cashmere, silk, poplin – her interesting use of crochet and hand painting as embellishment, the inspiration she derives from the Irish landscape and seascape, the essential romanticism of her vision and her use of literary and artistic allusion all combine to give her work a gentle and muted 'Irish' quality. This is a contemporary version of the same quality seen in a subtly coloured pleated linen Sybil Connolly dress.

'The Irish landscape is a great inspiration to me'

MARY GREGORY

Mary Gregory exports to Japan and has lately received a lot of interest from the UK to which she will soon export. She was asked by the Donegal wool firm Magee to design their first womenswear collection – a nice collaboration between Irish fabric producer and Irish designer.

Lynn Elliott of Lyn-Mar is another designer, predominantly of knitwear, whose career started in 1985. She is now doing extremely well, with 150 outworkers. She is an interesting designer who left school at fifteen, who had no formal training and who learnt pattern-making by trial and error. None of this is evident in her refined and finely textured award-winning work. It is the yarns which determine the style of her garments. Her work usually evolves to a new look about every two years or so. She has found it easier to export than it was initially to break into the Irish market, and sells to the US, Canada, Belgium and is about to attempt the UK market.

Michelle O'Doherty is one of the few fashion designers with a national reputation to have made her base in Northern Ireland, in Derry. Her work can be compared to Louise Kennedy's, but has its own qualities – it is perhaps less formal than Louise's although just as beautifully tailored and finished. The hallmarks of her soft tailoring are the very comfortable fit and fine finish. The wool she works with is fine and usually Italian, but the linen which she uses to effect is usually Irish.

PLATE 80 Outfit by Gertrude Sampson, 1995. Her originality is seen in both the design of the outfit and the styling of the image. (Photo: Barry McCall)

She trained at the University of Ulster and at the Royal College of Art in London, and then worked with Byblos. Four valuable years working in Italy for a design company were followed by a period in Paul Costelloe's design studio in Dungannon. This wide-ranging experience of the international fashion world has undoubtedly stood Michelle in good stead and made her return to her home town all the more viable.

Miriam Mone, from Armagh, was the *Late Late Show* Designer of the Year in 1995. Her confident, sharply tailored day wear, in plain strong colours, is her great strength. She is perhaps one of the most international of the young designers in outlook and style. Yellowhammer is the label of Susan Casey, who started her company, with no formal fashion training, in 1989. A second label, Sushi, was added in 1991. Brid Nihill is best known for her wonderfully extravagant evening dresses. Allicano is the label of Una O'Reilly, whose new label is selling ever more widely. Gertrude Sampson and Deirdre Fitzgerald both design strong, distinctive knitwear. Another new knitwear designer is Tim Ryan, who sells through Se Si.

Some of the most interesting Irish fashion developments of the 1990s have been in menswear. As the Irish editor of *Uomo Vogue*, Godfrey Deeney, puts it, Ireland has finally, in the 1990s, broken out of the traditional concept of tweed and rainwear. John Rocha's first menswear collection was in 1991, and he produced a striking collection for spring/summer 1996. Paul Costelloe, who made marvellous menswear in the early eighties, has produced new collections. The talented Nicky Wallace, who has great potential, but had business difficulties, is now sucessfully designing ranges again.

Pat McCarthy is thought of by many journalists as the most likely new international star of Irish fashion. He produced a range of women's clothes in the eighties, for export to the US. After he returned here from the US in 1991 he formed his own marketing consultancy in Dublin. He began to work closely with McNutts and other Donegal woollen weavers and with linen weavers to produce cloths with Irish characteristics but a soft and pleasing feel. These suit his designs which take their initial inspiration very much from traditional western seaboard dress, but which are essentially contemporary. His collections are sold in Ireland but appeal very much to the export markets of US and Europe. As many designers have found over the years, the Germans in particular like an ethnic, Irish fabric and style.

Overseas, Murray Scallon, produces a distinctively rich menswear collection for, at present, an Italian market. Many of the home-based menswear designers of high fashion avant-garde menswear, produce only for club-scene shops or make particular capsule collections for

Left:
PLATE 81 Trouser suit by 'Yellowhammer', whose designer is Susan Casey. (Photo: Ronan O'Raw) IMAGE Magazine September 1995

PLATES 82 and 83 Two images from Pat McCarthy's autumn/winter 1996 menswear collection. Pat's designs are contemporary but their inspiration is from rural, traditional Irish dress. His experiments with varying weaves and blends of fabric have resulted in garments whose feel, often unexpectedly soft, is a large part of their appeal. (Photo: Kip Carroll)

shows or for commission. Designers such as Terence Doyle, a Smirnoff award winner in 1991 and now a teacher in the Belfast Institute clothing department, are aware that only their more commercial designs are economically viable in Ireland.

DESIGNERS OF HATS AND JEWELLERY

Some of Ireland's most notable designers work in the field of costume accessories. Philip Treacy is probably the world's best-known milliner, and Slim Barrett's fashion metalwork is better known outside Ireland than within the country.

Philip Treacy, from Ahascragh, Co. Galway, is one of the most internationally famous of Irish designers. He is a milliner of startling technique, talent and originality. His Irish roots are important to him

as an individual, but have no obvious reference in his work which is both personal and international.

He went first to the Regional Technical College in Galway, then to NCAD from where he graduated with a first class degree. He won a British Council scholarship to do his MA in fashion and millinery at the Royal College of Art in London. Two celebrated milliners, Alan Couldridge and Kirsten Woodward, taught him, and he worked in the studio of another, Stephen Jones. He was asked to design hats by the highly talented British designer John Galliano, and was

PLATE 84 Terence Doyle's original menswear designs make an unexpected reference to tradition by the use of Aran stitch detail in his 1994 collection. (Photo: Rory Moore)

introduced to Shirley Hex, the doyenne of milliners and a superb teacher who saw Philip as a 'Rembrandt' of millinery. *Harper's and Queens* sponsored his final collection, and he was subsequently backed as the designer of hats for Bill Horseman's label, 'Right Impressions'.

He has, up to the present, designed hats for the collections of Rifat Ozbek, Norman Hartnell couture with Marc Bohan, Chanel, Versace and Valentino among others as well as having a host of private customers. His collections' work has won him the greatest fame. His hats are always a crucial part of the proportion of a designer's work – they are never merely accessories. The extravagant feather hats for Chanel of 1991, the tall pagoda-like hats for Ozbek in 1992, his Chinese creations for Valentino in 1993 all enhanced the garments with which they were worn and also excited almost as much editorial comment as the clothes.

Philip Treacy's hats can be exciting in shape, colour, and content, or wonderfully sculptural in simple abstract shapes. An example of the former is his extraordinary showpiece hat in the form of a huge black feather sailing ship, and of the latter his hat made for the Ulster Museum (*see* plate 85). His manipulation of feathers continues to be a strong feature of his work. He does not have any artistic pretensions, but interestingly sees hats as mathematical problems to be solved, and hat making as a craft.

Designers in Ireland have been quick to capitalize on the revival of the casual hat as practical and fashionable headwear. Cathy Shannon's designs are sophisticated, in a wide variety of materials from suede to

PLATE 85 Sculptural linen hat by Philip Treacy, made as a commission for the Ulster Museum in 1993. This simple, abstract shape is a fine contrast to the lavish feather extravaganzas with which Philip is most often associated.
Collection Ulster Museum

PLATE 86 Slim Barrett's metalwork is often hard to define. This waistcoat/necklace is the largest and most striking piece from his East of Paris collection of 1991. He often works with fashion designers to produce complemary pieces.
Collection Ulster Museum

swathed fabric to wool. Originally many of her hats were of a basic, if softened, cloche shape, which could be pulled on, rather than placed on the head. Now the shapes often have an Edwardian feel. Other successful hat designers include Rita Daly, whose hand-blocked, dyed and painted hats are immensely attractive, Jacinta Fahy of Wicklow Street, Linda Caulfield and Kathleen McAuliffe. Most of these sell in The Collective, the brainchild of jeweller Vivien Walsh. It was set up in 1993 to sell and promote Irish jewellery and accessories. The shop in the Powerscourt Townhouse Centre, Dublin, has expanded and now stocks the work of twenty-five accessories designers.

While the broad field of contemporary jewellery is outside the remit of this book it includes mention of jewellers who have worked with fashion designers for collections, or who generally work within a high fashion, costume-based context.

Slim Barrett, from Galway, has won international attention for his metalwork and jewellery. He has often worked with fashion designers such as Rifat Ozbek, Antony Price, John Rocha or Calvin Klein, who find his strong, innovative style complements their own work. His own designs can cross the border between jewellery and garments, as can be seen in the illustration of the Ulster Museum's waistcoat/ necklace which has matching cuffs (*see* plate 86). Killian Schurmann is primarily a glass maker, but his extravagant glass pins for Romeo Gigli's collection of 1987, perfectly complemented the rich, romantic clothes. Tom Binns has worked for Rifat Ozbek, for example in 1986, when his silver brooches were a focal point of the simple, puritan garments. Nuala Jamison from Lisburn, Co. Antrim, has an international reputation, being best known for her work in plastics and perspex. For many years she designed both jewellery and very distinctive buttons for Jean Muir's collections.

THE DESIGNERS – UPDATE

I am conscious that whatever I write now is likely to be out of date and overtaken by events by the time of publication. The continuing development of the top Irish designers not so far referred to in this chapter must be mentioned. I start with those who appeared in the February 1996 Brown Thomas Showcase of Irish Fashion Design. (If I seem to be labouring the 'Point' it is because this show, at which five supermodels worked, brought Irish fashion to its biggest ever national and international audience.)

John Rocha has just returned to the UK to show in London Fashion Week after two seasons in Paris, and has been welcomed back enthusiastically. His menswear collections have been attracting much attention. Colour has become increasingly important to him, and he continues to develop new fabrics, for example 'crackled' silk. In his own very nice phrase, he continues to '"portray" women as they wish to be seen'.

Paul Costelloe's empire has grown and his business is based more and more in England, especially after the opening of his flagship store in London and his winning of the important British Airways uniform

PLATE 87 One of Quin & Donnelly's particular design talents is the sharp styling of leather, so that its image is contemporary and fashionable. This suit dates from 1995. (Photo: Ursula Steiger)

PLATE 88 Cleverly textured dress by Claire Garvey whose work concentrates on the manipulation and embellishment of fabric. (Photo: Conor Horgan) IMAGE Magazine February 1995

contract in 1994. In his gentle unstructured designs, his recent use of handkerchief linen to make dresses was striking. His colour palette, recently predominantly brown toned, now includes sharp, citrus colours.

Louise Kennedy's fabrics are becoming ever more fluid and her simple, long-line dresses have become another trademark. Quin & Donnelly's work, which has in recent years been tailored and quite fitting, is now too more soft than formerly. They use large printed floral motifs in their current season.

Peter O'Brien, having already reworked the Aran, is now working with Carrickmacross lace, which should be an interesting development. His work continues to use beautiful fabric lavishly and to great effect, whether in tightly cut or billowing garments, as seen most effectively in the Point show.

Richard Lewis, Pat Crowley and Thomas Wolfangel remain as bastions of high quality ready-to-wear and made-to-measure standards. Thomas Wolfangel's tailored suits remain his most characteristic and profitable line, but his plainest dresses often show his tailoring skills at their best. Richard Lewis, too, is at his best when at his simplest, showing his skills in working with difficult fabrics to greatest advantage. His 'Guinness' collection of simple dark dresses of 1994 was highly praised. As his contribution to the Point show displayed, he is also capable of exuberance. Pat Crowley mostly now produces clean-cut, practical garments, but she too can still produce a lavish and stunning evening gown.

PLATE 18 White trouser suit by Miriam Mone, 1996, a good example of her tightly tailored style. (Photo: Barry McCall)

PLATE 19 A photo session on a Dublin rooftop illustrates Marc O'Neill's exploration of painted clothing, 1995. The image was planned in sketch form, shot in 15 separate takes, scanned to photo CD, digitally merged, retouched and adjusted for colour and focus.

(Photo: Eamonn McLoughlin, Graphic Artist: Marcus Gosling)

PLATE 20 A splendid Philip Treacy hat, 1991, worn by Linda Evangelista, made during his first year of working for Chanel. Patrick Demarchelier © Vogue, *Condé Nast Publications Inc.*

Photographs from the Brown Thomas Showcase of Irish Fashion Design at the Point, Dublin, 3 February 1996, in aid of ISPCC, Children of Chernobyl and Cradle.
The scale of this show and the presence of the supermodels generated much national and international publicity for Irish fashion.
(Photos: Barry McCall)

PLATE 21 *Paul Costelloe daywear, model Helena Christensen.*

PLATE 22 *Richard Lewis wedding outfit and Philip Treacy hat, model Naomi Campbell.*

PLATE 23 *Lainey Keogh knitwear, model Christy Turlington.*

PLATE 24 *Quin & Donnelly outfit, model Karen Mulder.*

PLATE 25 *Louise Kennedy outfit, model Helena Christensen.*

PLATE 26 *Marc O'Neill outfit, model Yasmin le Bon.*

PLATE 27 *Jen Kelly evening outfit, model Naomi Campbell.*

PLATE 28 *Peter O'Brien evening outfit, model Helena Christensen.*

PLATE 29 *John Rocha outfit, model Yasmin le Bon.*

PLATE 30 *Mary Gregory dress, model Karen Mulder.*

PLATE 31 A high-fashion French rendition of the Aran sweater by Jean Paul Gaultier, 1985. (Photo: Niall McInerney)

PLATE 32 Naomi Campbell wearing Lainey Keogh knitwear, 1994. (Photo: Chris Moore) New Generation Designer Show at Harvey Nichols, London.

Most knitwear designers' work continues to evolve rather than change dramatically season by season. Lainey Keogh and Edel McBride, continually experimenting with new yarns, keep to the forefront of fashion, as Lainey's impressive Point exhibits showed.

CLOTH, COLOUR AND CREATIVITY

The range and variety of fabrics and fibres available grows every year, and the competition between fabric producers intensifies. Mixtures of natural and manmade fibres, keeping the best qualities of both elements, become more and more sophisticated. It can often be hard to define certain fabrics as either natural or manmade – the two are no longer in opposition to each other. Since all designers have access to the same international range sold at the big fabric fairs, discernment is needed to buy fabric which is distinctive without being *outré*, or fashionable without being bland and overexposed. It can happen that an expensive designer may buy and make up the same fabric in the same way as a cheaper manufacturer. In winter 1995/6, for example, both Gianni Versace and Quin & Donnelly made similar dresses in the same black nylon fur, the chief difference being the price.

Consequently, many Irish designers now treat the purchase of fabric as only the first stage in its use for their designs. They choose a fabric for its inherent textural qualities, and then individualize it by painting, printing and dyeing. This work is often done in collaboration with another artist; for example, Lorraine Bowen works with Mary Gregory and Louise Kennedy; Lou Brennan, Nuala Goodman, and Clea van der Grijn with John Rocha; and Ian Hannon with Marc O'Neill. Very often the graphic work is the dominant design feature of a simply cut garment. Other means of personalizing a fabric are the insertion of other handwork, most usually crochet. Although it is also admittedly a contemporary international trend, it is tempting to see this tendency towards the embellishment of fabric as a continuation of a long tradition in Ireland. In the recent past, for example, Patricia Jorgensen was a forerunner in this type of collaboration. She worked in the same way with Ib Jorgensen in the 1970s, embellishing couture designs with hand painting, embroidery or appliqué. Richard Lewis, too, has used textile artists' work in his collections, notably the batik artist Bernadette Madden.

This element of customized craft in dress is perceived by the fashion editor of the *Sunday Times*, Paula Reed (from Limavady, Co. Derry) to be one of the long-term contributions of Irish fashion to the international fashion world. She sees it as a part of the natural processes favoured by the eco-movement.

Some of the most interesting work of fashion students and young designers in Ireland has featured their development of new finishes of fabrics, and indeed it is often hard to know whether to define them as textile or fashion designers. Alan McCool, Wendi Hoey and Claire Garvey are some of the many examples of this new breed. Wendi Hoey's deconstructed work won her the Smirnoff International Fashion Award in 1993 (*see* plate 70). Claire Garvey won the Irish section of this award in 1990. After finishing her NCAD degree and an MA in Russian, and studying costume and textiles at the Goskina Institute of Cinematography in Moscow, she has returned to Ireland where she now creates dresses, headwear, collars and shawls from dyed, embroidered and heat-treated velvets and other fabrics.

Undergraduate work often includes specialized textile production, or unusual materials. These can range from the beautiful bonded and heat-treated garments of Liam Greer of Limerick Regional Technical College to the car-seat-belt garments of Kelvin Feeney of Dublin's NCAD, the Irish Smirnoff winner of 1994. Teachers such as Patricia Keilthy feel that more resources are needed for research and development into fabrics. Certainly a unit such as the London Royal College of Art and Design's Design Research Department where art, science and technology merge as one discipline, would be an exciting and timely development in Ireland.

Frequently all these methods of making individualistic clothes produce garments that cross the boundaries between high fashion and applied art. The Crafts Council of Ireland's 1996 'Adornments' show underlined this relationship between garment, textile and craft, and exhibited the work of several designers who feature in this book.

The same cross-over between commerce and art can be seen in the work of Irish craftsmen weavers, mostly from the Guild of Spinners Weavers and Dyers, which is sometimes used in fashion. It is seen too in the work of specialist commercial weavers of wool and linen who produce fashion fabrics. The developments in linen production have already been mentioned. One of the most interesting developments in wool weaving has been the increasingly vivid use of colour. Previously bright colours were most typically used on their own or mixed in tweeds, but they are often now used in contrasting checks. Indeed, producers of these patterns such as Castleisland and Tim Roberts are sometimes given broad hints by the more conservative buyers to tone down their colours to the more traditionally Irish soft natural tones. Tim Roberts is an interesting example of a successful one-man weaving operation. He trained originally as a damask weaver then graduated from the University of Ulster, and now is based in Newtownards, County Down.

He has two distinct markets: a developed home market for accessories and garments made from his wools, typically of large brightly coloured checks; and a developing export market of fabric for *haute couture* designers who appreciate their sophistication, such as Gianni Versace, Ted Lapidus and Peter O'Brien of Rochas. His first significant export order of tweed and cotton was from the London house of Lachasse which had design links with Ireland in the 1930s, '40s and '50s. His label Little Patrick Street (a mythical thoroughfare) helps spell out his Irish/urban roots – a good example of definition by label.

At the other end of the scale from all these producers of what the world sees as quintessentially Irish cloth, it might be salutory to remember that one of Ireland's biggest fabric exports is the product of the denim factory which supplies this cloth to all of Europe.

IRELAND'S INFLUENCE

The basic characteristics of contemporary Irish fashion are highlighted when one looks at the influence Irish designers have had on their international peers. It is predominantly Ireland's knitwear and fabrics which have inspired European, American and Japanese designers.

Jean Paul Gaultier's reinterpretation of Aran in autumn 1985 was the most newsworthy borrowing of the tradition. A more consistent admirer of the Irish knitwear tradition is Kenzo Takada, the Japanese designer, who was, with Issey Miyake, one of the first and most influential of the Japanese designers in Paris – his shop, 'Jungle Jap', was opened as early as 1970. His clothing was influential but as Colin McDowell has put it: 'His real impact was made with his revolutionary and totally contemporary knitwear, which revitalized the knitwear industry.'[3] He is an inveterate traveller and in the mid-1980s was having brightly coloured, Aran-style sweaters machine made in Co. Mayo. Ireland's knitwear industry also produces work for designers such as Armani and Romeo Gigli, despite Italy's having an equivalent but more mechanized home knitwear industry of its own.

The designers who from time to time use Irish knitwear designs, such as Perry Ellis, frequently use Irish wools in the same collection. American designers in particular can produce a very relaxed and contemporary version of *le style Irlandais*. Periodically the French adopt this style themselves. Dior's menswear collection of autumn/winter 1995 was inspired by Irish colours and fabrics and called the *Irlandaise* collection.[4] French couturiers have often used Irish cloth. Italian designers also use Irish tweeds, made into what are seen as traditional English styles.

International designers are now just as likely to use Irish fabrics as their Irish counterparts. The most important of all the European fabric fairs is Premier Vision held in Paris, and most medium to large Irish wool and linen producers market their wares there. An order from one of the big UK or American ready-to-wear designers is economically more important, and therefore more desirable, than the sale of smaller quantities to the home market.

CONCLUSION

It is hard to avoid a certain feeling of guarded optimism in contemplating the prospects of Irish fashion over the next few years. At home and abroad, established and new designers are now as acutely aware of the business world and the challenges of new technology as they are of their own design compulsions. There are enough successful designers to give heart and hope to newcomers. The business of fashion will never be easy, as even the most successful can testify. As well as creative and business talent, there are other requirements. Designers must have the stamina for the long hours required, especially before a collection or show. They must be philosophical both in the face of difficulties, such as replenishing sold-out stock or correcting production mistakes, and of disasters, from the hi-jacking of the lorry carrying vital cloth for a collection to the theft of a complete collection at the last minute before a show – as happened to Michelle O'Doherty and Louise Kennedy respectively. They must be able to cope with the time-lapse between payment out for cloth and labour and payment in for retail garments. They must be able to talk to the media and sell themselves, and yet find time for quiet creativity.

Indeed, as I have talked to the many designers over the course of researching this book I have often felt and remarked that only obsession would make any sane person pursue a life in the fashion business. Invariably, the designers have agreed. The satisfaction of seeing a personal vision made real is one of the few rewards of which they can be certain.

Irish designers have a great sense of camaraderie, which I am not at all sure is a universal quality in fashion designers. They are, to make broad generalizations, very family-oriented, and many more have families of their own than is usual in such a high-pressure job. Perhaps this is an element which has kept them more grounded in reality and less precious than some of their peers in other countries. A high proportion of Irish designers are women, and one wonders too, if the vibrant creativity which used to be expressed in domestic textiles, especially quilts, by Irish women of the past has some resonance in the almost passionate response to fabric and colour of their contemporary sisters.

The compact size of Ireland and its relatively small population put constraints on designers' activities. No home-based Irish designer, for example, can hope to have any sort of franchising operation, and the few designers of international reputation who have launched perfumes, such as Sybil Connolly and Paul Costelloe, have not kept up this production. Hopefully John Rocha's new store, due to open in 1996, will be the first single-designer store to thrive in Dublin, and it may well be the start of a new and welcome trend. Ireland's size does have some advantages as far as creative collaboration is concerned. It is easy to meet and link up with other designers and like-minded people in such a country, and it is a notable feature of most Irish fashion designers that their design interests extend far beyond their own field.

PLATE 89 A graceful, simple and contemporary use of crochet by Pat Crowley in 1989. (Photo: Kip Carroll) IMAGE Magazine July/August 1989

Relatively few people in Ireland are more than two generations away from rural life and many have family homes or favourite countryside to which they often return. These rural roots affect even the most sophisticated designers, and very few have not at some time or to some degree derived some inspiration from the landscape, colours, or traditions of the Irish countryside. In most countries fashion is a completely urban phenomenon, and all the attributes of rural life such as traditionalism, conservatism and, often, poverty are completely antithetical to the very concept of fashion. Irish designers have managed continually to recreate the inspirational characteristics of country living so that their designs both retain a freshness and interest, and also avoid the potential dangers of stage Irishness.

A sense of romanticism also features in the work of many Irish designers of any age at home or abroad. Irish fashion is not, with a few exceptions, hard-edged. It often has a sense of allusion: historic, literary or cultural. These characteristics, along with the feeling for fabric, especially Irish fabric, that has been a recurring theme in this book, give some sense of unity to the work of Irish designers. Unity is probably too strong a word for the diffuse feeling that there may be some linking sympathies in their work. This feeling is best expressed by a phrase of that wonderful phrase maker, Medbh McGuckian in her poem: 'The Flitting',[5] where garments are described as a 'fraternity of clothes'.

> I've been carried from one structure to another
> On a chair of human arms, and liked the feel
> Of being weightless, that fraternity of clothes . . .

APPENDIX 1: AWARDS

LATE LATE SHOW: Designer of the Year

Late Late Show Fashion awards are divided into categories for coats, suits, knitwear, day dresses, separates/co-ordinates and after-six/wedding outfits. An overall Designer of the Year is picked from the winner of one of these categories. Two new categories were added in 1995: Student Designer and Fashion Industry Achievement award.

1982 Michael Mortell
1983 Michael Mortell
1984 Michael Mortell
1985 Ritzy
1986 Mariad Whisker
1987 Robert Jacob
1989 Louise Kennedy
1991 Quin & Donnelly
1993 Mariad Whisker
1995 Miriam Mone

SATZENBRAU FASHION AWARDS – DESIGNER OF THE YEAR

1988 Richard Lewis
1989 Mariad Whisker
1990 Pat Crowley
1991 Paul Costelloe
1992 Louise Kennedy

SMIRNOFF YOUNG DESIGNER OF THE YEAR AWARD

Northern Ireland
1991 Judith McCaul
1992 Lisa Blanchflower
1993 Sharon Cunningham
1994 Catherine McAllister
1995 Julie Beattie

Republic of Ireland
1990 Claire Garvey
1991 Gillian Gallagher
1992 Paula Hughes
1993 Wendi Hoey
1994 Kelvin Feeney
1995 Ngan Ling Kwok

ULSTER MUSEUM IRISH DESIGNER PURCHASES

Spring/summer 1993 –
John Rocha
Autumn/winter 1993 –
Lorcan Mullany
Spring/summer 1994 –
Lainey Keogh
Autumn/winter 1994 –
Louise Kennedy
Spring/summer 1995 –
Quin & Donnelly
Autumn/winter 1995 –
Mary Gregory
Spring/summer 1996 –
Marc O'Neill

Ulster Museum International Designer Outfit purchases (initiated 1983) also include outfits by Irish designers Paul Costelloe (autumn/winter 1984), Michael Mortell (spring/summer 1985) and Mariad Whisker (spring/summer 1989).

APPENDIX 2: COSTUME COLLECTIONS IN IRISH MUSEUMS

The following institutions have significant collections of fashionable costume. Most smaller and specialist museums also hold costume, some of it very fine.

National Museum of Ireland, Kildare Street, Dublin. From 1997 all departments except Antiquities move to Collins Barracks, Benburb Street, Dublin 7. Tel: Dublin 6777444. Costumes, textiles and accessories are held in the departments of Antiquities, Art and Industry and Irish Folklife. The bulk of the costume collection comprises English and Irish material. The eighteenth-century collection is particularly strong, and twentieth-century material includes some Celtic Revival costume and a small representation of Irish designers.

Springhill Costume Collection, Springhill, Moneymore, Co. Londonderry. Tel: 016487 48210. This National Trust property houses an impressive collection of some 2,300 costumes dating from the eighteenth century to the present day. The highlight of the collection is a splendid Court Mantua of 1759–60.

The Rothe House Museum Costume Collection, Kilkenny Archaeological Society, Rothe House, Kilkenny. Tel: Kilkenny 22893. This collection of several hundred items, dating from the mid-eighteenth century to the 1970s, was founded on the collection given to the society by Mr and Mrs Toler-Aylward about 1990. Since then further material has been added.

The Ulster Museum, Botanic Gardens, Belfast, BT9 5AB. Tel: 01232 383000. The Ulster Museum's collection of costume has been rebuilt since the former collection's destruction in 1976. It dates from the early eighteenth century to the twentieth century. An important element of this new collection of about 3,500 items is twentieth century international *haute couture* and contemporary fashion. Every season a 'High Street' outfit from a shop in Belfast, an International Designer outfit which demonstrates a key look of that season and an Irish Designer outfit, is bought.

The Ulster Folk and Transport Museum, Cultra, Holywood, Co. Down. Tel: 01232 428428. The bulk of the museum's collection of costume and accessories dates from 1840 to 1910, with some more recent specimens. Everything is of Ulster provenance or manufacture. Most of the dress is female – there are particularly fine mid- to late-nineteenth century examples – with some children's dress and occupational costume.

APPENDIX 3: SOME GOVERNMENT AND TRADE BODIES WHICH ASSIST THE FASHION INDUSTRY IN IRELAND

An Bord Tráchtála, the Irish Trade Board, Merrion Hall, Strand Road, Sandymount, Dublin 4. Tel Dublin 2695011. The State agency with responsibility for promoting and developing trade. It provides trade information, support services, and development advice and help.

Clothing Development Centre Limited, Kennedy Enterprise Centre, Kennedy Way, Blackstaff Road, Belfast BT11 9DT. Tel: 01232 431300. Workspace, production facilities, office services, advice and information offered to those wishing to start or develop a clothing business.

Crafts Council of Ireland, HQ, Powerscourt Townhouse Centre, South William Street, Dublin 2. Tel: Dublin 6797368. The national economic development agency for the crafts. Its objectives are to develop the market for Irish craft at home and abroad and to encourage the highest standards of excellence in design and making. It does this through providing marketing facilities, exhibitions, training and information. It has a gallery space and shop at the above address and organizes 'Showcase', the annual exhibition of craft and fashion at the Royal Dublin Society Exhibition Halls at Ballsbridge, Dublin.

Craftworks, Linenhall House, 17/19 Linen Hall Street, Belfast BT2 8AA. Tel: 01232 236334. Advice, training and retail outlet for crafts-based producers, including those working in the clothing and textile business.

Forbairt, Head Office, Glasnevin, Dublin 9. Tel: Dublin 6602244. The agency providing state support services to Irish industry. Support is provided across a range of commercial activities including management, product development, finance and a broad range of technological services.

LEDU, Local Enterprise Development Unit, LEDU Regional Office, 25/27 Franklin Street, Belfast BT2 8DT. Tel: 01232 242582. The small business agency in Northern Ireland which gives financial, counselling and training help to businesses at all stages of development.

IDA Ireland, Wilton Park House, Wilton Place, Dublin 2. Tel: Dublin 6686633. IDA Ireland has national responsibility for securing new investment from overseas in manufacturing and international services sectors and for encouraging existing foreign enterprises in Ireland to expand their businesses. State-sponsored organization with national responsibility for the furtherance of industrial development in Ireland.

The Irish Fashion Group, Chairman: Victor Buckley, Stylex Ltd, Mornington Park, Artane, Dublin 5. Tel: Dublin 6799443. This was set up in the mid-1970s and is a co-operative group of manufacturers who came together to merchandise and show as a unit. It can supply its members with information about design, fashion forecasting, technology, etc.

IDB Industrial Development Board (NI), IDB House, 64 Chichester Street, Belfast BT1 4JX. Tel: 01232 233233. Set up in 1982, the Northern Ireland branch of the British Overseas Trade Board. Financial and marketing support, and information given to companies with over fifty employees.

Irish Linen Guild, 5c The Square, Hillsborough, Co. Down BT26 6AG. Tel: 01846 689999. Founded in 1928, the Irish Linen Guild represents all sectors of the Irish linen industry. It acts to maintain high standards within the industry and to promote Irish linen in national and international textiles and clothing markets.

The Irish Knitwear Exporters Guild, Holbrook House, Holles Street, Dublin 2. Tel: Dublin 6612182. Established in 1985 as a promotional and marketing body, IKEG now represents 23 knitwear producing companies. It runs a design award scheme which places ten design graduates for six months with members of the IKEG.

Society of Designers in Ireland, 17 Merrion Square, Dublin 2. Tel: Dublin 2841477. Formed in 1972, the SDI is a professional association of designers of different disciplines who practise in Ireland. Its activities include seminars, exhibitions, publications, training and design competitions.

APPENDIX 4: DIRECTORY OF DESIGNERS

This directory is intended to give basic information about a broad selection of Irish fashion designers and manufacturers, most of whom are mentioned in the text. The entries are formulaic, except where information has proved difficult to obtain. Where a company is still in production, a contact address and telephone number is listed. This may be factory, salon, workshop or a primary retail outlet, as appropriate.

Aine at Sasha (Aine McDonnell, fashion designer). Trained at Grafton Academy of Dress Designing, since 1994 has designed her own label of individualistic designs for 'Sasha'. Sasha, 32 Henry St, Dublin 1. Tel: Dublin 8731166/8731371

Alison-Jayne Couture (Alison-Jayne Matthews), bridal, evening and theatrical designer. Trained University of Ulster, Faculty of Art and Design, started own label in 1991. Awards include UK 'Live Wire' Business award. Studio 407-411, McAvoy House, 17a Ormeau Avenue, Belfast BT2 8HD. Tel: 01232 325444

Allicano (Una O'Reilly, fashion designer). Trained at National College of Art and Design, Dublin, started own label in 1993. Her work is distinguished by the innovative use of hand-textured fabrics. Allicano is exported to the US, Japan, Kuwait, the UK and France. 15 Carrickhill Rise, Portmarnock, Co. Dublin. Tel/fax: Dublin 8463752

Ambers, Michel. Manufacturing company, has had Greta Scotland as designer since 1978. The firm has been a finalist in every *Late Late Show* awards presentation. They export most of their products to Britain, Europe and the US. MA International Ltd, 98 Lower Clanbrassil Street, Dublin 8. Tel: Dublin 4544361.

Annett, Margaret, made-to-measure and ready-to-wear designer. Born Newcastle, Co. Down, trained Manchester College of Art and Belfast College of Art and Design. Started own label in 1982. In 1992, she went on British Council-funded trip to Kenya as advisor to its clothing industry. Her designs are 'classic and timeless'. The ready-to-wear range is exported to the US and Canada. 50 Bloomfield Avenue, Belfast BT5 5AE. Tel: 01232 738938

Avoca Handweavers. Family run firm whose business was originally based at the mill at Avoca, dating from 1723, which was run from 1927 to the late

1960s by the Wynn sisters, who supplied handwoven tweeds to Irish designers. The firm now produces clothing ranges and has five stores, all in scenic parts of Ireland. Kilmacanogue, Bray, Co. Wicklow. Tel: Dublin 2867466

Brenmar, Jon, fashion design company, designers Liz Spillane from Cork and Catherine Gibbons from Devon, started 1995. Both have worked for a variety of manufacturing companies. 25 Henry St, Kenmare, Co. Kerry. Tel: Killarney 41138

Carroll, Carmel, fashion designer. With no formal training, she started her own label in 1984, and was a founder member of the Design Centre. The Design Centre, Powerscourt Townhouse Centre, Clarendon Street, Dublin 2. Tel: Dublin 6795718

Casey, Susan, see Yellowhammer.

Cavanagh, John, born 1914. Trained with Edward Molyneux in Paris and London 1932–40. Served in Intelligence Corps in Second World War, then travelled through the USA studying fashion promotion. Assistant to Pierre Balmain 1947–51. Opened own house 1952. Elected to Incorporated Society of London Fashion Designers 1952, Vice Chairman 1956–9. Known for elegant day and evening wear, society wedding dresses

Clarke, Jack, 1908–74, coat and suit manufacturer and retailer. Started 'J. N. Clarke and Sons' in 1934, opened 'Richard Alan' in Grafton St, Dublin 1935. Began to export his 'Country Wear' label to North America in 1947, the first Irish manufacturer to do so. Sybil Connolly established and ran the couture section of the business, and became its designer until 1957. 'Richard Alan' is still in business, but the factory was closed in 1972

Cleo Irl Ltd, founded by Catherine Ryan in 1936, was originally best known as a retail outlet for home-spun handknits from the west of Ireland. Now run by her daughter, Kathleen Joyce, who has designed for the firm since 1955, it is a largely export business producing knitwear and clothing from natural Irish fabrics and yarns. Cleo Irl Ltd, 18 Kildare Street, Dublin 2. Tel: Dublin 6761421

Clodagh, fashion and interior designer, trained at the Grafton Academy of Dress Designing, began own label in 1956. Worked as journalist, boutique owner and designer (with a successful export trade to the US) until she left Ireland for Spain in 1972. Thereafter lived and worked in New York as an architectural and interior designer. Her designs are strongly Irish in inspiration. Clodagh Design International, 365 First Avenue, New York, NY 10010–6503. Tel: 212 614–9125

Connolly, Sybil, couturière, born Wales 1921. Trained at Bradleys, London, until return to Ireland at outbreak of war. Joined 'Richard Alan' 1940 and started couture workroom, for which, from 1952 to 1957, she was designer. Showed collections in US from 1953. Established own house in 1957. Particularly noted for her innovative use of Irish fabrics and lace, especially for her hallmark pleated linen. Has produced fabric designs for Brunschwig et Fils and, since the 1980s, has produced ranges of Tipperary glass, Nicholas Mosse pottery and parian porcelain by Tommy Daly for Tiffany's of New York. Awards include 1958 'Woman of the Year' in Great

Britain, frequent appearances on 'Best Dressed Women of the World' list, Honorary Doctorate from National College of Art and Design, Dublin, 1991, Special Achievements award at Satzenbrau Fashion Oscars, 1988. 71 Merrion Square, Dublin 2. Tel: Dublin 6767281

Connon, Geraldine, fashion designer of made-to-measure and ready-to-wear daywear. Born Larne, Co. Antrim. Founder member of Fashion Business Centre, Belfast. Trained at Belfast College of Art and Design. Winner of 1993 and 1995 Satzenbrau Fashion Showcase Northern Ireland Designer award. 52 Glenarm Road, Larne, Co. Antrim BT40 1BD. Tel: 01574 272430

Connor, John, fashion designer, born Belfast, 1962, trained Rupert Stanley College, Belfast, Ulster Polytechnic and St Martins School of Art, London. Worked as designer and illustrator in London before starting designing for Erreuno Italy in 1986. After various related design posts he is now, since 1995, responsible for the fabric research and realization of 5 lines of 'Krizia'

Costelloe, Paul, fashion designer, born 1945. His Blackrock education was followed by a year on a business course at Rathmines, a year at a bacon factory at Cappoquin, then a year at the Grafton Academy of Dress Designing. He then went to the Chambre Syndicale in Paris to study design, followed by a couple of years working for Jacques Esterel. Another couple of years were spent successfully designing in Milan before Paul went to the US. He worked for a short time with Anne Fogerty, but soon returned to the north of Ireland where in 1979, in partnership with Robert Eitel, a local businessman, he set up the manufacture of his own label in the Strelitz factory in Moygashel, Dungannon. Designs three collections – the 'Paul Costelloe Collection', 'Dressage' and 'Dressage Jeans'. His use of Donegal tweeds and wools and Irish linen became his trademark. Awards include Fil d'Or, 1987, 1988, 1989, Satzenbrau Designer of the Year, 1991, nomination for British Designer of the Year, 1989. Designed British Airways uniform, 1994. Paul Costelloe International Ltd, Main Road, Moygashel, Co. Tyrone. Tel: 01868 722291

Coughlan, Jim, fashion designer, born Cork, 1974, trained at National College of Art and Design, Dublin. Worked with Vivienne Westwood as a student, then spent three years as freelance designer in Milan before taking responsibility for the daywear section of ready-to-wear at Christian Lacroix

Crowley, Pat, couturière, born 1933. Worked with Irene Gilbert for seven years before opening her own business in 1967, originally concentrating on knitwear. Since the 1970s she has turned to designing wedding dresses, then other day and evening wear. Winner of Satzenbrau Fashion Oscar, 'Designer of the Year', 1990. Shop and salon at 3 Molesworth Place, Dublin 2. Tel: Dublin 6615580.

Cullen, Cyril, knitwear designer, self-taught. Started own business in 1973 after accepting a large commission. His designs, originally colourful, have become more muted in tone since he began to use Jacob sheep wool extensively. Cyril Cullen Knitwear, Carrick-on-Shannon,

Co. Leitrim. Tel: Carrick-on-Shannon 20100

Davies, Donald, fashion designer and manufacturer. Began making his distinctive fine wool shirts and dresses in 1955 at his home-cum-factory and workroom, Charleville, Enniskerry, Co. Wicklow. For over 20 years he had an extremely successful home and export business. His shirt-dress became a design classic

Digby Morton, see Morton, Henry Digby

Donnellan, Michael, see 'Michael'

Doolan, Eily, fashion and knitwear designer, born London 1953, trained at Camberwell School of Arts and Crafts, Ravensbourne College of Art and Design and Croydon College of Design and Technology. Started her own label in 1977 in Kilkenny, where until the early 1980s she worked with her first husband, John Rocha. At first best known for her lavish evening and wedding dresses, she now concentrates more on knitwear designs, and has worked on a consultancy basis for knitwear companies. She also works for the United Nations Industrial Development Organization. Rosslea Studio, Adelaide Road, Bray, Co. Wicklow. Fax: Dublin 2867486

Doyle, Terence, menswear designer, born Belfast, trained at the Belfast Institute of Higher Education. Has shown his couture collections of menswear at a wide range of prestigious shows in the North and South of Ireland. Now works as lecturer and freelance design consultant. 55 Springfield Avenue, Belfast BT12 7BA. Tel: 01232 311498

Elliott, Lynn, see Lyn-Mar

Evans, Maureen, designer and consultant, who was to a large extent responsible for the standardizing of the sizes of handknit sweaters in the 1940s and 1950s. Her own knitwear designs were successful contemporary adaptations of traditional stitches and forms. For many years she worked with Kennedy's of Ardara.

Fanagan, Elizabeth, milliner. Trained with Renée Pavy in London, Jean Barthet in Paris and at Bergdorf Goodman's workshops in New York. Her own salon in Dublin was open from 1962 to 1965

Fitzgerald, Deirdre, knitwear designer. Trained NCAD, with Arts Council scholarship. Started own label in 1991, specializing in women's knitwear, hand-worked in cotton, chenille, silk and silk/wool blends, often with textured trimmings. Exports to UK, USA, Europe and Japan. The Design Centre, Powerscourt Townhouse Centre, Clarendon Street, Dublin 2. Tel: Dublin 6795718.

Garvey, Claire, fabric and fashion designer. Trained at National College of Art and Design, Dublin, and studied costume and design at the Goskina Institute of Cinematography, Moscow. Won the Smirnoff Young Designer of the Year award, Republic of Ireland, 1990. Makes garments and accessories from hand-treated and dyed fabrics. 136 Griffith Avenue, Dublin. Tel: Dublin 8371232

Gilbert, Irene, couturière, d. 1985. Trained in London, opened her first shop in 1947 in Dublin and her salon in 1950. She retired in 1968. During her design career she was particularly noted for her fine tweed daywear and draped and Irish lace evening wear. She was a most accomplished cutter and finisher. She showed successfully in the US, was involved in film design and in 1966 and 1967 produced the third and fourth Irish Fashion Fairs.

Grant, Mary, fashion designer, born Dublin 1967. Trained at Barbara Bourke College of Fashion. Started own label 1993. Fluid separates for women are typical designs. Powerscourt Townhouse Centre, Clarendon Street, Dublin 2. Tel: Dublin 6795718

Green, John, milliner. Born Belfast 1929, trained at Paddington Technical College, and with Renée Pavy in London and Jean Barthet in Paris. Produced hats for Sybil Connolly's collections in 1955 and 1956 and for her tour of Australia in 1957. From 1961 to 1975 he had his own salon in Wellington Street, Belfast

Gregory, Mary, fashion designer. Trained at the Grafton Academy of Dress Designing, founder member of The Design Centre in 1984. Her work is fluid with a subtle colour palette, and hand-finished details such as crochet or painting typify her work. The Design Centre, Powerscourt Townhouse Centre, Clarendon Street, Dublin 2. Tel: Dublin 6795718

Hoey, Sharon, fashion and wedding dress designer, born Dublin. Trained at the Grafton Academy of Dress Designing. Started own label in 1980, specializing in made-to-measure wedding gowns. Now also exports wholesale to England and the Netherlands. Won *Late Late Show* Wedding Dress category 1993. 19 Upper Mount Street, Dublin 2. Tel: Dublin 6762772

Hoey, Wendi, designer, born Drogheda. Trained at National College of Art and Design, Dublin. Winner of the 1993 Smirnoff International Fashion awards in Sao Paolo, Brazil, for her design 'Ecdysis'. Now works as a freelance designer. 44 Glenmore Drive, Drogheda, Co. Louth. Tel: Drogheda 30595

Hourihan, Jimmy, designer and manufacturer. Best known for his Irish tweed coats and suits which he has exported successfully to the US and England since the start of his business in 1955. 6 Lee Road, Dublin Industrial Estate, Glasnevin, Dublin. Tel: Dublin 8300033

Inis Meáin Knitting Company (Director, Tarlach de Blacam), knitwear company set up in 1977. Produces high fashion garments for predominantly export market, using computer technology and a variety of yarns. Inis Meáin, Aran Islands, Co. Galway. Tel: Galway 73009

Jackson, Maggie, see Maggi Knits

Jorgensen, Ib, born 1935, Denmark. Came to Ireland with family in 1949. Trained at Grafton Academy of Dress Designing, taking diplomas in dress design and tailoring. In 1955 'Michael' awarded him first prize in a National Industrial and Agricultural Development Association (NIADA) competition. 1955–7 chief designer for Nicholas O'Dwyer. Opened own couture house 1958, which he closed in 1994. Designed for 'Mattli', 1980s. He twice designed the Aer Lingus uniform in the 1970s, and also designed historic theatrical costume. Beautiful finishing and tailoring, and lavish evening dresses, often painted or embroidered by his first wife, Patricia Jorgensen, typified his designs.

Jorgensen, Patricia, textile designer, trained at National College of Art and Design. Worked in design studios in Ireland and the Netherlands. Her fashion design work has most notably been the hand-painted and embroidery designs produced for Ib Jorgensen garments. Most typical were the embroidered jackets, which she still occasionally produces. 24 Kingram Place, Fitzwilliam Place, Dublin. Tel: Dublin 6611094

Kelly, Jen, couturier. Born in Derry. Starting with a business course, he became involved in theatrical design. After that he went to the College of Design and Marketing, and then to NCAD where he left with a first class degree in fashion in 1983. Afterwards did design work, e.g. for ROSC, the international contemporary art show in Dublin, lectured, worked in Los Angeles, then set up a successful couture business in 1989. Designed the costumes for *Riverdance*. Jen Kelly Designs, 38 Molesworth Street, Dublin 2. Tel: Dublin 6769844

Kenna, Raymond, designer and manufacturer, who during the 1950s produced striking day and evening wear often using Irish tweeds in unusual colours and weights

Kennedy, Louise, fashion designer. Born Dublin, trained at Grafton Academy. Established own business in 1986, successfully expanded to UK and other export markets, late 1980s and '90s. Designed President Robinson's inauguration jacket. Winner of *Late Late Show*'s awards, Designer of the Year 1989, Suit and Coat Designer of the Year 1991, Suit Designer of the Year 1993, Satzenbrau Designer of the Year 1993. 22 South William Street, Dublin 2. Tel: Dublin 6719564

Keogh, Lainey, knitwear designer, born Oldtown, Co. Dublin, 1957. Self-taught, her professional knitting career began in 1984. Her knitwear, chunky and vividly coloured in the 1980s, has become softer and lighter in the 1990s. She is successful both commercially and as a continually inventive designer. Awards include the *Prix de Couer*, given by Christian Lacroix in Monte Carlo in 1989. 24 South Anne Street, Dublin 2. Tel: Dublin 6793299

Lewis, Richard, couturier, trained at the Grafton Academy of Dress Designing, started fashion career in 1965. Best known for his draped jersey outfits and his fitted tailoring. His awards include a Satzenbrau award for his contribution to Irish fashion over 25 years in 1990, Satzenbrau Designer of the Year Oscar in 1988, and a *Late Late Show* award, Day Dress category in 1991. 22 South Frederick Street, Dublin 2. Tel: Dublin 6797016

Libra, manufacturing company, designer Dolores Beggan, has for over twenty years developed a worldwide export business. Libra Designs, 17–19 Sycamore Street, Dublin 2. Tel: Dublin 6711288.

Little Patrick Street (Tim Roberts, fabric designer and weaver). Trained as damask weaver, then at University of

Ulster Textile Design Department. His woollen fabrics have both a home market, mostly made up into accessories, and an export market, often to couturiers. 10a Hiberia Street, Holywood, Co. Down BT18 9JE. Tel: 01232 422828/fax: 01232 427801

Lorna Doone (designer Joan Doogue). Trained Grafton Academy of Dress Designing and College of Fashion and Technology, Oxford Circus, London. After design work in England, returned to Ireland and started children's wear company in 1990. Since 1993 has designed women's wear, typically knitwear and linen separates. The Design Centre, Powerscourt Townhouse Centre, Clarendon Street, Dublin 2. Tel: Carlow 47749, mobile 088 607317

*Lyn-Mar (*Lynn Elliott, knitwear and fashion designer). Self-taught, began her own company in the mid-1980s after being involved in a co-op. Has a distinctive use of yarn and texture. Winner *Late Late Show* awards, Knitwear category, 1993, After-Six category, 1995. The Design Centre, Powerscourt Townhouse Centre, Clarendon Street, Dublin 2. Tel: Dublin 6795718

McBride, Edel, trained Limerick Regional Technical College. Started own business in 1987. Her designs combine Irish/Celtic and Japanese inspiration, and show experimental use of yarns. Her awards include two Satzenbrau special awards and a *Late Late Show* award, Knitwear category, 1995. Convoy Woollen Mill, Convoy, Co. Donegal. Tel: Donegal 47507

McCarthy, Pat, menswear fashion designer, trained in fashion and business in Manchester. With partners produced a range of women's clothes for sale in the US, late 1980s. After his return to Ireland first produced his own collection in 1995, using traditional-looking fabrics in new blends and weaves, aimed primarily at the export market. 37 North Great Georges Street, Dublin. Tel: Dublin 8726504

McNamara, John. Fashion designer. Trained at the Grafton Academy of Dress Designing, Kingston Polytechnic, Surrey, and as an assistant to Ib Jorgensen. Started own label in 1988 in Limerick designing After-Six and Evening Wear. Won 1990 Shannon Region Fashion Designer of the Year award. 6 Quinlan Street, The Crescent, Limerick

Magee, Winnie, rainwear designer, born Glenavy, Co. Antrim. Trained London College of Fashion and Belfast Institute. Her range of 'waterproof' linen coats have been very successful in both the home and export markets. Ards Business Centre, Jubilee Rd, Newtownards, Co. Down BT23 4YH. Tel: 01247 819787 Ext 211

Maggi Knits (Maggie Jackson, knitwear designer). Trained at Belfast College of Art and Design, started own label in 1977. Founder member of Northern Ireland Fashion Designers Association. Best known for her work with linen yarn, in a variety of stitches and textures. Awards include Northern Ireland Young Business and Professional Woman of the Year (runner up in Great

Britain) and Guinness/Satzenbrau Special Award for Design Excellence, 1994. Design Studio 307, Fashion Business Centre, McAvoy House, 17A Ormeau Avenue, Belfast BT2 8HD. Tel: 01232 236777

'Michael', couturier Michael Donnellan, 1915–85, born Ballinlough, Co. Roscommon. Studied medicine before war service and training at the British Fashion Institute. Worked as suit designer at Lachasse before opening own house in Carlos Place, London. His work was marked by the purity of its line and perfection of finish. During the 1960s was design consultant for Marks & Spencer. Retired 1971

Millar, Joan, knitwear designer, born Belfast. With no formal training, began own company in 1982. 'Updated classic' designs in hand and machine knitting in a range of yarns. Has a thriving export business. Killiney, Co. Dublin. Tel: Dublin 2852343. Fax: Dublin 2855116

Molyneux, Edward (Captain), 1894–1974, couturier. Born England of Irish parentage. Worked with the London couturière 'Lucile' as sketcher, and after service in the First World War started his own house in Paris in 1919. His elegant, restrained designs were very successful with a wide clientele including royalty and theatrical stars. He designed for the stage, notably for Noel Coward's plays. From the mid-1930s he was based in London and was a founder member of the Incorporated Society of London Fashion Designers. After the Second World War he returned to Paris. He retired in 1950, but made a brief unsuccessful comeback in 1964, the only failure in a widely respected design career

Mone, Miriam, fashion designer, born Armagh, trained Limerick Regional Technical College. Started own label in 1990 after winning the Grolsch Question of Style award. Other award include *Late Late Show* Designer of the Year award, 1995, and *Late Late Show* award for coats, 1993. Sharply tailored suits are typical of her designs. The Design Centre, Powerscourt Townhouse Centre, Clarendon Street, Dublin 2. Tel: Dublin 6795718

Morrison, Kathryn, now mostly bridal designer. Born Bangor, Co. Down. Took a science degree, then trained at Belfast Technical College. Started own label in 1982, and was initially best known for her leather designs. Studio 309, McAvoy House, 17a Ormeau Avenue, Belfast BT2 8HD. Tel: 01232 312185

Mortell, Michael, fashion designer, born in Mallow, Co. Cork, trained at Belfast College of Technology, St Martins School of Art, London and Hollings College, Manchester, before working with Ib Jorgensen for two years. He started his own label in 1978 and had shops in Dublin and Brussels in the mid-1980s. In 1990 he decided to concentrate production on his signature raincoats. He also produces the 'Michael Mortell Country' range. His awards include *Late Late Show* Designer of the Year titles for 1982, 1983 and 1984. 1 Cope Street, Dublin 2. Tel: Dublin 6711193

Morton, Henry Digby, 1906–83. Born Dublin, trained in Art and Architecture at the Metropolitan School of Art, Dublin, 1926–9, then worked at Lachasse of London until he opened his own couture house in 1934. Founder member of Incorporated Society of London Fashion Designers 1942, Vice President 1955–6. Retired 1973. Particularly known for his fashionably cut suits

Mulcahy, Neilli, couturière. Trained at the Grafton Academy of Dress Designing and with Jacques Heim in Paris. Opened her own house in 1952 and until her retirement in 1970 ran a successful couture house which specialized in Irish fabrics

Mullally, Sheila, couturière. After a period as house designer for Elizabeth James, started her own house in 1964. Specialized in finely coloured tweeds, mostly for the American market

Mullany, Lorcan, couturier and fashion designer. Born Bansha, Co. Tipperary, trained at the Grafton Academy of Dress Designing. Worked with Hardy Amies and Bill Gibb, and while working for Ronald Joyce, also in London, began to work on his own collection. Joined Bellville Sassoon in 1987 as designer of ready-to-wear collections. Especially noted for his dramatic ballgowns. Bellville Sassoon–Lorcan Mullany, 18 Culford Gardens, London SW3 2ST. Tel: 0171 581 3500

Nihill, Brid, fashion designer. Started own label in 1989. Best known for evening wear in the grand style. The Design Centre, Powerscourt Townhouse Centre, Clarendon Street, Dublin 2. Tel: Dublin 6795718

O'Brien, Peter, fashion designer. Born Dublin 1951, trained St Martin's School of Art, London. Worked in New York and in Paris with Givenchy and Dior before becoming house designer at Chloé. Since 1990 has been designer for 'Rochas'. His 'ready-to-wear luxe' is typically of beautiful, rich fabrics, often with discreet but opulent embellishment. Rochas, 33 rue Francois 1er, 75008 Paris. Tel: Paris 4723 5456

O'Doherty, Michelle, fashion designer. Trained at University of Ulster and Royal College of Art, London. Worked for 'Byblos' in London, for the 'Iceberg' label in Italy and for Paul Costelloe in Dungannon before starting her own label in 1992. Her speciality is easy fitting well-tailored separates and dresses. The Studio, 23 William Street, Derry BT48 6ED. Tel: 01504 372132

O'Donnell, Mary, couturière. Born in Donegal. After apprenticeship to dressmaker in Ireland, went to New York in 1950 and after some time working as an alteration hand at Bergdorf Goodman, enrolled at the Traphagen Academy of Dress Design, then spent two and a half years at Mainbocher. On return to Ireland worked with Sybil Connolly, then opened her own house in 1963. Uses fine Irish fabrics. Much of her work has Irish literary and artistic allusion. 12 Avondale Lawn, Carysfort Avenue, Blackrock, Dublin. Tel: Dublin 2880794

O'Neill, Marc, fashion designer. Born 1970, trained Institute of Education, Dublin, NCAD, de Montfort University, Leicester. Awarded Society of Designers in Ireland student bursary, 1993, named Fashion Graduate of the the Year by Society of Designers in Ireland, 1993. One of A-Wear's label designers since 1995.

A-Wear, Henry Street, Dublin 1. Tel: Dublin 8724529

Pink Inc (Carole Cairns and Colleen Tilson, fashion designers). Both trained at Belfast College of Art and Design. Colleen Tilson set up Colleen Tilson Designs, and, with Carole Cairns, set up Pink Inc in 1984. It was in operation until 1991. Its designs had distinctive, strong shapes. By 1986, they had their own retail outlet in London, initially at Hyper Hyper. Colleen Tilson, now Colleen Cairns, designs from 5 Old Grand Jury Manor, Saintfield, Co. Down. Tel: 01238 511479

Petersen, Kay, couturière and boutique owner. She opened her boutique 'Anna Livia' in Dublin's Dawson Street in the mid-1960s, selling garments typically of Irish tweed and crochet, often vividly coloured. Its name revealed her Joycean interests. From 1978 she worked for some time with Thomas Wolfangel in his new boutique

Quin & Donnelly (Carolyn Donnelly and Liz Quin, fashion designers). Both trained at Grafton Academy of Dress Designing. Carolyn Donnelly was a fashion writer with the *Irish Press* for seven years and started studio/shop 'Ritzy' in 1978. She was joined by Liz Quin in 1979 and 'Ritzy Design Studios' was formed. After financial difficulties, late 1980s, they were invited to design for A-Wear, under their own label, in 1989. Since then they have been very successful in producing good value, well-tailored and interesting collections, often with unusual mixes of fabrics and textures. Awards include *Late Late Show* Designer of the Year 1985 (as Ritzy) and 1991, and five category awards. Quin & Donnelly, 10–11 Moore Lane, Dublin 1. Tel: Dublin 8726933

Ramsay, L. S. Ramsay of Dublin (designers Helen McAlinden and Linda Byrne), is a long-established firm which has a high fashion profile, and has a strong export market especially to the UK. L.S. Ramsay Ltd, 17/21 Foley Street, Dublin 1. Tel: Dublin 8740672

Regine, manufacturing company (designers Fran Nolan and Ann Marie Keegan), was started in 1974 with the aim of bringing European fashion trends to Ireland. Winner of *Late Late Show* fashion award, Suit category, 1983. Regine Ltd, 13–14 Dame Court, Dublin 2. Tel: Dublin 6798122

Reynolds, Vonnie. Throughout the 1970s Vonnie Reynolds produced highly romantic, lavish evening wear of fine fabrics often trimmed with Irish lace or crochet, from her Co. Clare base

Roberts, Tim, see Little Patrick Street

Robins, Glynis, knitwear designer. Trained at Grafton Academy of Dress Designing and Fashion Institute of Technology, New York. Started her own label 1984. Now produces separates as well as knitwear for women, men and children. Awards include *Late Late Show* Fashion awards, Special award – Runner-up 1987 and Knitwear category 1989. 20 Railway Road, Dalkey, Co. Dublin. Tel: Dublin 2856827

Rocha, John, fashion designer. Born in Hong Kong, trained at Croydon College of Design and Technology, came to Ireland in 1977 at invitation of CTT and ran his own label business from Kilkenny until the early 1980s. His next label, Chinatown, began in 1984 and wound up in 1987. He moved to Milan to work under licence to produce his own collections and revived the Chinatown label which was developed after his return to Ireland in 1989. From 1990 to 1994 he worked under licence to the Brown Thomas A-Wear Group. He was named 'Designer of the Year' in 1993 at the British Fashion Awards, and showed his collection in Paris for the first time in 1994. His garments are typically simple in shape, of fabrics which have been treated or embellished to give them distinction. Both Celtic and Oriental influences are apparent. Menswear range first shown 1991. The firm exports to over 20 countries and is about to open a flagship store in Dublin. Business headquarters 12–13 Temple Lane, Temple Bar, Dublin 2. Tel: Dublin 6772011

Sampson, Gertrude. Knitwear designer. Born 1968, Co. Limerick. Trained as a science teacher before starting her own label, after working to private commissions, in 1992. Uses yarn and texture in original and creative ways. 'Platform', Creation Arcade, Dublin 2. Fax: Dublin 6777380

Scallon, Murray, fashion designer. Born Irvinestown, Co. Fermanagh, trained NCAD, has designed for 'Erreuno', Milan, since 1989. His own collection of menswear was first shown in June 1995, available at present only in Italy

Shannon, Cathy, milliner. Born Scotland, came to Northern Ireland 1968. Originally a teacher, with no formal training, she started her own millinery label in 1989, producing soft, easily pulled-on, mostly fabric hats in which the worked textile is the dominant feature. 1 Desart Lane, Armagh BT61 8AR. Tel: 01861 524257

Sheena L (Sheena Lyons, fashion designer). Trained Grafton Academy of Dress Designing. Started own label in 1992. Designs for the 18–40 age group, ready-to-wear and made-to-measure for private commissions. 10/11 Exchequer Street, Dublin 2. Mobile: 087 454960

Smyth and Gibson of Belfast (Wendy Smyth, shirtmaker). High quality linen and cotton poplin shirts made primarily for export markets, initially to London. Craftworks, Bedford Street, Belfast. Tel: 01232 236334

Stacpoole, Michelina, knitwear designer. Born Italy, trained at couture house and at Krizia in Rome. To Ireland early '60s, and set up Hollypark Knitwear with Heather Cohane, 1966. Set up own business at Pallaskenry, Co. Limerick, 1972. Occasional teacher at Limerick Regional Technical College. Winner of International Award from the International Wool Secretariat. Classic tailored knitwear designs in European tradition. The Stacpooles, Knitwear, Antiques, Main Street, Adare, Co. Limerick. Tel: Limerick 396409

Treacy, Philip, milliner. Born Ahascragh, Co. Galway. Trained at NCAD and at the RCA in London. One of the world's best known milliners, he has been house milliner for Chanel, Valentino, Rifat Ozbek, Hartnell, among others, sells a diffusion range, and has a large private clientele. Winner, Accessory Designer of the Year 1991 and 1992, British Fashion Awards. Salon at 67 Elizabeth Street, Belgravia, London, SW1W 9PJ. Tel: 0171 259 9605

Tully, Una, retail designer of the 1950s who had worked in the US, where she received much of her design inspiration

Waldron, James, born Ballyhaunis, Co. Mayo 1965. Trained Limerick Regional Technical College, NCAD. Worked for Luciano Soprani (who designs for the Basile and Gucci labels as well as his own) before joining Giorgio Armani five years ago. Now senior design assistant to Sr Armani

Wallace, Nicky, fashion designer, born 1952, Wexford Town. Trained Jacob Kramer, Leeds College of Fashion. Started first own label 1981/2, ceased trading 1989. Relaunched label 1993, and launched new diffusion label 'Southern Shores' in 1995. Exports to the US, Italy, France and Germany. Best known for menswear, now also designs for women. 15 South Anne Street, Dublin 2. Tel: Dublin 6776560

Whisker, Mariad, fashion designer. Born Belfast, trained at Manchester College of Art. Her beautifully proportioned, simple designs depended on the perfect choice of fabric, often linen or viscose. After twenty years in the fashion business she left Ireland for Los Angeles in 1995. Awards include the Fil d'Argent, Monte Carlo, for her designs in linen 1989, Satzenbrau Designer of the Year 1989, *Late Late Show* Designer of the Year 1993

White, Henry. Henry White & Co. Ltd (designer David White) is a long-established (founded 1934) clothing manufacturing firm which produces women's wear and men's outerwear. The quality of tailoring is very high. The firm was one of the first to export to the UK, from the late 1940s. 15 South Summer Street, Dublin 8. Tel: Dublin 4533611

Wolfangel, Thomas, couturier. Born Stuttgart, 1935. Handcraft tailoring apprenticeship, 1949–52; won awards from Tailor and Cutting Academy. Came to Ireland 1956, opened own couture house 1966. His hallmark is his detailed tailoring. Salon and workroom at 99 Lower Baggot Street, Dublin 2. Tel: Dublin 6604069

'Yellowhammer' is the label of Susan Casey, who started her company with no formal fashion training in 1989. A second label, Sushi, was added in 1991. The company exports to the UK and Norway. *Late Late Show* award winner, Daydress category, 1995. Yellowhammer, Textile House, 3–5 Johnsons Place, Dublin 2. Tel: Dublin 6707939

NOTES

Chapter 1

1. Fynes Moryson, born 1566, went to Ireland in 1600 as secretary to the Lord Deputy, and wrote an account of his travels: Fynes Moryson, *An Itinerary* (James MacLehose and Sons, 1907), Vol. IV, p. 236.

2. The standard book on historic Irish dress is Mairead Dunlevy's *Dress in Ireland* (B.T. Batsford, 1989).

3. William Good, 1566, quotation incorporated in vol. ii of 1722 edition of Camden's *Britannia*, p. 1420, quoted in H.F. McClintock, *Old Irish Dress* (Dundalgan Press, Dundalk, 1950), p. 74.

4. *Calendar of State Papers of Ireland 1588–92*, ed. H.C. Hamilton, Longman et al, 1885, pp. 192–3, quoted in Dunlevy's *Dress in Ireland*, p. 4.

5. *Calendar of the State Papers relating to Ireland of the Reign of Elizabeth, 1598–1599*, ed. Ernest George Atkinson (Eyre and Spottiswoode et al, 1895), p. 251, quoted in Dunlevy's *Dress in Ireland*, p. 4.

6. See Jack McCoy's article 'The Ulster Coat' in *The Irish Arts Review*, Vol. 2, No. 4 (1985), pp. 18–23.

7. One of the best and most concise accounts of Aran knitting is Deirdre McQuillan's *The Aran Sweater* (Appletree Press, Belfast, 1993).

8. Catherine Ryan was initially inspired to the purchase of Aran and Connemara sweaters because garments made of handspun wool did not require her precious wartime clothing coupons. Her business benefited greatly from the arrival of American tourists in Ireland in the 1950s, and thrives to this day, with a healthy export market.

9. Robinson, Tim, *Stones of Aran: Labyrinth* (The Lilliput Press, Dublin, 1995), p. 316.

10. John Derricke's illustrated account *The Image of Ireland with a Discouerie of Woodkarne* was published in 1581, after his return from Ireland to England.

11. The Dublin Society, later the Royal Dublin Society, was founded in 1731 for 'improving Husbandry, Manufactures and other Useful Arts'. The Sciences were later added to its remit. By 1761 it received a large annual grant from the Irish parliament to help fulfil these aims, and gave practical help to the textiles industries. Premiums and grants were given to the beleaguered silk industry. In 1765 it opened a retail silk warehouse which gave a 10 per cent premium on all Irish-made silk.

12. The Elliott family was involved in poplin weaving in Dublin from the early eighteenth century. Thomas Elliott and Sons was established in 1879 and closed

in 1970. Its fabric inspired many Irish couturiers of the 1950s and 1960s. Because Elliott's hand looms produced narrow 27-inch width fabric they had to adapt their designs, often producing panelled garments.

13. Dun Emer (in English 'Emer's Fort') was named after Emer, the wife of Cu Chulainn, hero of the old Irish epic tales. She was famed for her skill in weaving and embroidery.

Chapter 2

1. *Harper's Bazaar* of March 1956 had printed on its cover 'Spring Collections Paris London Dublin Italy'.

2. A very large establishment, with an established apprenticeship system which had a large royal and colonial clientele. The Dowager Queen Mary and Princess Marina of Kent were among its number.

3. *Sunday Evening Press*, 1955.

4. Mary Delany née Glanville (1700–88), letter writer and artist. Wife of Patrick Delany, Dean of Down.

5. Irene Gilbert designed the costume for *Shake Hands with the Devil* featuring Dame Sybil Thorndike, Dana Wynter and Glynis Johns in 1959.

6. Aer Lingus have always used Irish designers and manufacturers for their air hostess uniforms, which are redesigned every three to five years. Irene Gilbert, Neilli Mulcahy, Ib Jorgensen and Paul Costelloe have all been commissioned. The uniforms have to reflect Aer Lingus' image and be smart and practical.

7. *See* Robert O'Byrne's article, 'Couture for a Countess: Lady Rosse's Wardrobe', *Irish Arts Review Yearbook 1996*, vol. 12, pp. 157–63.

8. Donald Davies dresses were among the first to be advertised as garments which could be worn all day, from morning to evening. One rather unlikely suggestion in 1957 was that the dress in question could be worn 'dusting, sweeping and doing the household chores, gathered into a plain belt for shopping or afternoon wear, or cinched with kid and diamante circle for dinner parties or cocktails'.

9. The Lachasse connection with Ireland, which began coincidentally, continues, thanks to the generous help which the present director, Mr Peter Crown, gives to University of Ulster surface design student projects. The firm has always taken a keen interest in fabric and pattern research.

10. Gerd Hay-Edie, now in her eighties, is a remarkable woman who is one of Ireland's most influential designer weavers. Born and trained in Norway, she worked for the Rural Industries Bureau in the 1930s, and after living for some time in China she settled with her family in Northern Ireland, and founded Mourne Textiles at Killowan near Rostrevor. She was often amused at the disappointment of visiting journalists who hoped to find a little old lady clinging to the side of the mountain with her loom instead of the efficient small factory she built up – a not uncommon reaction of the urbanite visiting the country at that time.

Chapter 3

1. In 1960 a group of eminent Scandinavian designers was invited to visit and assess industrial design in Ireland. As a result of the recommendation in its report *Design in Ireland* that an 'Irish Institute of Visual Arts' be set up, Kilkenny Design Workshops was established in the stables

and coachhouse of Kilkenny Castle.

2. Mrs Kennedy's 1970 portrait by Aaron Shickler depicts her in a pleated linen dress and another Shickler portrait of her with her children, painted in the early years of her widowhood, also shows her wearing a Sybil Connolly pleated linen outfit.

3. Eileen Brogan from Armagh took over from Sheila Mullally as designer at Elizabeth James.

4. She held a fashion show on one eve of 'Bloomsday' (the annual commemoration in Dublin of 16 June, the day on which the action of James Joyce's *Ulysses* takes place), with outfits named 'Finnegan', 'Martelloe', 'Proteus', etc, for an audience which included Sylvia Beach, Madame Jolas and a variety of Irish literary figures, who all seem to have thoroughly enjoyed it. I am indebted to Professor Edna Longley of Queens University Belfast for this reference.

5. Jean Muir (1933–95) was most renowned for her fine jersey dresses, which she tailored into fluid but structured garments which have become design classics.

6. Madame Grès (1910–94), like Jean Muir, was most associated with jersey. Her designs were draped and sculptural, often compared to the styles of Ancient Greece.

7. Quoted in Colin McDowell, *McDowell's Directory of 20th Century Fashion* (Frederick Muller, London, 1984), p. 234.

8. The companies she founded there include Clodagh Design International and Clodagh Design Works. Her interior design work for companies and individuals has been very successful. Using 'environmentally sound materials, modern technology and the ancient art of Feng Shui' (a philosophy of the placing of objects) she designs spaces, furniture, textiles and is returning to fashion.

9. All seven of the long-established Belfast department stores were shut by the early 1990s.

10. His life has to some extent come round full circle, for he has worked again for the government in the Department of Foreign Affairs, helping set up hand-knitting industries in Lesotho.

11. Mrs Phyllis Seigne, who used to model for Sybil Connolly and Irene Gilbert in the 1950s, says that at that time one kept quiet about such activities.

Chapter 4

1. Azzedine Alaïa, born in Tunisia, is a designer to whom 'the base of all fashion is the body', and who has consistently produced beautifully cut, very tight-fitting garments. He was especially influential in the mid-1980s.

2. The progression of 1980s fashion from romantic to figure-revealing to almost aggressively strong-shouldered was remarkably like that of the equally recession-hit 1930s.

3. Romeo Gigli, born in 1951 in Italy, produces clothes of distinctive proportion, in subtle but rich colours. His soft shoulder line with low-cut, tight sleeves was a stark contrast to the wide, strong shoulders of the mid- to late 1980s.

4. Giorgio Armani, born in Italy in 1935, designs understated clothes which although seemingly 'unstructured' and loose are in fact beautifully cut, of perfectly chosen, light fabrics. This popular combination of qualities has made him enormously influential.

5. He won three Fil d'Or awards in Monte Carlo, given by the International Linen Council for his linen designs, in 1987, 1988 and 1989.
6. *Irish Times*, 1 December 1987.
7. The grandmother of the Cullen family who run the large manufacturing company West End Knitwear was Mrs Kate O'Shea who commercially marketed her handknits in the nineteenth century.
8. Yohji Yamamoto, born in Japan in 1943, designs heavily textured, asymmetrical, draped, pleasing but non-glamorous clothing. His influential designs sell worldwide.

Chapter 5

1. This was a collaboration between the Fashion Business Centre, Nottingham Trent University, Scottish Enterprise and the GTTA (Garment and Textile Technology Association). As a group it provides market intelligence information which is transferred to data base format. The range of information covers sources of raw materials, design expertise, packaging, CMT services, market movements, fashion forecasting, modelling agencies, EC initiatives, etc, etc.
2. Coras Tráchtála, the Irish Export Board and the Irish Goods Council combined to form the Irish Trade Board, An Bord Tráchtála, in 1991.
3. She is now Group Fashion Director of the Brown Thomas Group, into which A-Wear is subsumed.
4. Spinning of flax throughout Europe has been reduced to 25 per cent of all European companies' capacity, which will only be increased to 50 per cent in 6 months if the market improves.
5. Breaking the large Southern hemisphere markets of Australia, New Zealand, South America and South Africa would at least double the demand for linen which is primarily a summer cloth, but tariffs prevent this. The linen business output is further dictated by specific worldwide tariffs – for example, linen blend going to the United States, still a big market, must be at least 52 per cent pure linen or import tariffs rise from 3 to 17 per cent to protect the US manmade fibre businesses.
6. The most internationally renowned Irish fashion journalist was Carmel Snow, 1887–1961, fashion editor of US *Vogue* 1921–32 and influential editor-in-chief of US *Harper's Bazaar* 1932–56.

Chapter 6

1. Mary Robinson had a distinguished legal career before her unexpected but very popular election as Ireland's first woman head of state.
2. *Riverdance – the Show* is based on the seven-minute interval act at the 1994 Eurovision Song Contest, held in Ireland. Bill Whelan wrote the music and the choreographer Michael Flatley and Jean Butler were the principal dancers in a performance which had stunning impact and has revitalized Irish traditional dance.
3. McDowell, Colin, *McDowell's Directory of 20th Century Fashion* (Frederick Muller, 1984) p. 183.
4. As an example of French couturiers' fondness for Ireland, Yves St Laurent used a shamrock against a red background for his New Year message to his customers in the January 1996 edition of *W* magazine.
5. *The Flower Master* (Oxford University Press, 1982), p. 48.

BIBLIOGRAPHY

Most information for this book came from newspaper and magazine files or was given directly by designers, journalists, agents, retailers, photographers, fabric producers, college teachers and all the other professionals who work in the fashion business in Ireland. The following are some general and specific reference books.

Brown, Terence. *Ireland: A Social and Cultural History 1922-1985,* Fontana Press, London, 1985.

Coleridge, Nicolas. *The Fashion Conspiracy*, Mandarin, London, 1989.

Connolly, Sybil. *Irish Hands: The Tradition of Beautiful Crafts*, Hearst Books, New York, 1994.

Crawford, W.H. *The Irish Linen Industry*, The Ulster Folk and Transport Museum in conjunction with the Irish Linen Guild, 1987.

Cullen, L.M. *An Economic History of Ireland since 1660*, Batsford, London, 1972.

de Breffny, Brian (general ed.) *Ireland: A Cultural Encyclopaedia*, Thames & Hudson, London, 1983.

Dunlevy, Mairead, *Dress in Ireland*, Batsford, London, 1989.

Ewing, Elizabeth. *History of 20th Century Fashion*, Batsford, London, 1992.

Flügel, J. C. *The Psychology of Clothes*, International Universities Press, New York, 1966.

Foster, R. F. *Modern Ireland 1600–1972*, Allen Lane/Penguin, London, 1988.

Hollander, Anne. *Seeing through Clothes*, Viking, New York, 1978.

Howell, Georgina (ed.). *In Vogue: Six Decades of Fashion*, Allen Lane/Penguin, London, 1975.

Lapidus, Ted and Proctor, Lynn. *Fashion and Anti-Fashion: An Anthropology of Clothing and Adornment*, Thames & Hudson, London, 1978.

Larmour, Paul. *The Arts and Crafts Movement in Ireland*, Friars Bush Press, Belfast, 1992.

Laver, James. *Taste and Fashion from the French Revolution to the Present Day*, G. G. Harrap, London, 1945.

Longfield, Ada. *Guide to the Collection of Lace*, National Museum of Ireland, Dublin.

Lurie, Alison. *The Language of Clothes*, Heinemann, London, 1981.

McClintock, H. F. *Old Irish and Highland Dress*, Dundalgan Press, Dundalk, 1950.

McDowell, Colin. *McDowell's Directory of 20th Century Fashion*, Frederick Muller, London, 1984.

McQuillan, Deirdre, *The Aran Sweater*, Appletree Press, Belfast, 1993.

Moryson, Fynes. *Itinerary*, James MacLehose & Sons, 1907.

O'Boyle, Elizabeth. *The Irish Flowerers*, Ulster Folk Museum and Institute of Irish Studies, Queen's University, Belfast, 1971.

O'Dowd, Anne. *Common Clothes and Clothing 1960-1930*, National Museum of Ireland, Dublin 1990.

O'Hara, Georgina. *Encyclopaedia of 20th Century Fashion*, Thames & Hudson, London, 1989.

O'Neill, Timothy. *Life and Tradition in Rural Ireland*, J. M. Dent & Sons Ltd, London, 1977.

Reade, Linda. *Aranwear and Tweed*, Johnston & Bacon, Edinburgh and London/Zircon Publishing Ltd, Dublin, 1973.

Reynolds, Mairead. *Some Irish Fashions and Fabrics* c. *1775–1928*, National Museum of Ireland, Dublin, 1984.

Robinson, Tim. *Stones of Aran: Labyrinth*, The Lilliput Press, Dublin, 1995.

Rutt, Richard. *A History of Hand Knitting*, Batsford, London, 1987.

Wilson, Elizabeth. *Adorned in Dreams: Fashion and Modernity*, Virago Press, London, 1985.

INDEX

Black and white illustrations are designated by *italic* type; colour plates by **bold** type